AF884765

RISK PROFILING AND TOLERANCE: INSIGHTS FOR THE PRIVATE WEALTH MANAGER

Edited by Joachim Klement, CFA

CFA Institute
Research
Foundation

Statement of Purpose

CFA Institute Research Foundation is a not-for-profit organization established to promote the development and dissemination of relevant research for investment practitioners worldwide.

Cover photo credit: Lost Horizon Images / Cultura collection / Getty Images

ISBN 978-1-944960-46-9

CONTENTS

CE Qualified Activity CFA Institute

This publication qualifies for 3 CE credits under the guidelines of the CFA Institute Continuing Education Program.

BIOGRAPHIES

Joachim Klement, CFA, is the head of investment research at Fidante Partners, where he focuses on research on listed investment companies and investment themes in alternative asset classes. Previously, he was head of thematic research at Credit Suisse Private Bank and chief investment officer of Wellershoff & Partners Ltd. In those roles he worked with private banks, family offices, and institutional investors to develop asset allocation strategies and identify thematic investment opportunities across all asset classes. Before joining Wellershoff & Partners, Mr. Klement was head of the UBS Wealth Management Research strategic research team, with responsibility for thematic research within UBS Wealth Management globally and the equity market and sector strategies. Mr. Klement has a master's degree in mathematics from the Swiss Federal Institute of Technology, Zurich, and a master's degree in economics and finance from the Universities of Zurich and Hagen, Germany.

Michael M. Pompian, CFA, is the founder and chief investment officer of Sunpointe Investments, a multifamily office investment consulting firm headquartered in St. Louis, Missouri. He was formerly a partner at Mercer Investment Consulting for 10 years, and was the national segment leader for the private wealth business. Prior to joining Mercer, Mr. Pompian was a wealth management advisor with Merrill Lynch and a private banker with PNC Private Bank. He has been quoted in *Money*, *The New York Times*, and other media outlets, including Bloomberg and CNBC, and is the author of four books: *Advising Ultra Affluent Clients and Family Offices* (Wiley 2009); *Behavioral Finance and Wealth Management* (Wiley 2006); *Behavioral Finance and Wealth Management,* 2nd edition (Wiley 2012); and *Behavioral Investor Types* (Wiley 2013). Mr. Pompian has a BS in management from the University of New Hampshire and an MBA in finance from Tulane University.

John E. Grable teaches and conducts research in the Certified Financial Planner Board of Standards undergraduate and graduate programs at the University of Georgia. Prior to entering academia, he worked as a pension/benefits administrator and later as a registered investment adviser. Dr. Grable was the founding editor of the *Journal of Personal Finance* and the cofounding editor of the *Journal of Financial Therapy*. His research interests include financial risk tolerance assessment, behavioral financial planning, and financial planning help-seeking behavior. Dr. Grable has published more than 100 peer-reviewed papers and co-authored several financial planning textbooks. He currently writes a finance and economics column for the *Journal of Financial Service Professionals* and serves as a co-editor for *Financial Planning Review*.

Elke U. Weber is the Gerhard R. Andlinger Professor in Energy and the Environment and professor of psychology and public affairs at Princeton University. Her research models decision making under risk and uncertainty and time delay from a psychological and neuroscience perspective. Dr. Weber is past president of three societies (Neuroeconomics, Judgment and Decision Making, and Mathematical Psychology) and a fellow of the American Psychological Association, the Association for Psychological Science, and the Society for Experimental Psychology. She was elected to the German National Academy of Sciences and to the American Academy of Arts and Sciences, and recently received the Distinguished Scientific Contribution Award from the Society for Risk Analysis.

Greg B. Davies is an expert in applied behavioral finance, decision science, and financial well-being. The combined entity provides behavioral consulting and develops decision-support tools to help people (and organizations) across the financial services industry make better decisions. Previously, as head of behavioral-quant finance at Barclays, he started the banking world's first behavioral finance team, which he led for a decade. Dr. Davis is an associate fellow at Oxford's Saïd Business School, a lecturer at Imperial College London, and the author of *Behavioral Investment Management*. He has a PhD in behavioral decision theory from Cambridge.

FOREWORD

Bob Dannhauser, CFA
Head, Private Wealth Management
CFA Institute

Client risk tolerance is fundamental to the successful achievement of client objectives, but it is also a concept that hasn't always been well-defined or well-integrated into the wealth management process. Individuals may have capacity for risk given a healthy level of assets relative to potential future claims on those assets and yet may have very little tolerance for risk taking, given their past experiences, psychological makeup, or degree of intimidation from the unknown contours of capital markets. Wealth managers often confront compounded complexities of client risk tolerance when addressing differing attitudes toward risk among spouses or family members, requiring reconciliation or at least education about how different attitudes toward risk might affect the ability to realize financial and life goals. And accounting for client risk tolerances continues to figure prominently on regulatory agendas that seek to minimize mis-selling episodes that subject clients to unintended and unwelcome degrees of volatility or loss.

The focus in recent years of CFA Institute Research Foundation on several facets of client risk tolerance is, therefore, quite welcome as a companion to innovations in the marketplace that introduce technology and structured frameworks to what had often been a series of less formal conversations between adviser and client. This compilation of briefs from CFA Institute Research Foundation should serve as an excellent resource to practitioners, sharpening understanding of the different dimensions that shape what we summarize as "risk tolerance," as well as suggesting a basis on which to evaluate some of the commercial tools available that purport to organize and summarize client attitudes toward risk. An adviser's ability to investigate clients' tolerances for risk knowledgeably and sensitively is essential not only to craft appropriate investment solutions but also to develop the candor and quality of relationship that will best serve clients and advisers alike in dynamic times. Practitioners are well-served by this important compilation from CFA Institute Research Foundation that addresses the issues that matter in the foundational work of assessing client tolerances for risk.

PREFACE

Investing Is Rational, Money Is Emotional

Ever since the advent of modern portfolio theory, professional and retail investors alike have struggled with the practical implementation of the theory. Although implementation is straightforward in many instances, the optimal portfolio of an investor depends on, among other things, her individual risk aversion. Identifying and measuring risk aversion is far from easy.

Investment theory assumes a rational investor does make a logical trade-off between the expected return and risk of a portfolio of investments. But investors are inherently human; hence, emotions will inevitably come into play. This is particularly true for less sophisticated investors who are not trained in finance and who lack experience with investments. Retail investors and high-net-worth individuals may be emotional about their lifetime savings, yet their advisers often find it difficult to assess how these emotions will be expressed in future financial decisions.

This difficulty should come as no surprise, because as human beings we are often surprisingly bad at identifying emotions. For instance, take a look at the picture below. Can you see the fear and terror in the woman's face? It makes you wonder what scares her enough to elicit such a vivid reaction.

Photo credit: Bloomberg/Getty Images

At the end of this preface, you will find a zoomed-out version of this picture that provides more context about the woman's facial expression. Indeed, the picture does not show a fearful woman but, rather, the tennis player Serena Williams winning the 2008 US Open Tennis Championship.

This example shows us two important things:

- How we interpret situations may depend on our perspective. A close-up provides more detail but less context than a broader perspective. Many investments share the same characteristics. Think about equity investments. Looking at stock market gyrations on a daily basis provides a lot of detail about share prices and the news that drives them, but it also increases perceived risk. Our emotions are running high when we look at the daily price swings; therefore, we perceive equity investments to be riskier than money market investments, for example. If we zoom out and look at the long-term performance of equity investments, however, they may be perceived as less risky and as the ideal assets for saving for long-term financial goals, such as a retirement nest egg.
- Our interpretation of emotions depends heavily on context. The same facial expression can be interpreted as fear and terror on the one hand and as extreme joy on the other hand, depending on the context given to us. In her book *How Emotions Are Made: The Secret Life of the Brain* (Houghton Mifflin Harcourt, 2017), Lisa Feldman Barrett explains in detail the scientific evidence that has been uncovered in recent years that emotions heavily depend on the context in which they are experienced. The previous example was taken from her book with permission.

If risk aversion and willingness to take on risk are driven by emotions and we as humans are bad at correctly identifying them, the finance profession has a serious challenge at hand—how to reliably identify the individual risk profile of a retail investor or high-net-worth individual.

In a series of CFA Institute Research Foundation briefs, we have asked academics and practitioners to summarize the current state of knowledge about risk profiling in different key areas.

In my introductory piece, I lay out the existing framework and challenges of risk profiling. Regulators increasingly demand that asset and wealth managers reliably identify such crucial ingredients of an individual risk profile as experience with and knowledge about financial investments and the ability to cope with losses. I also demonstrate that the current practice of risk profiling is often woefully inadequate for the job at hand.

In the second part of the series, behavioral finance expert Michael Pompian, CFA, demonstrates how finance has learned from psychology over the last four decades to identify stylized behavioral biases and deviations from so-called rational investor behavior. More importantly, however, he provides practical examples and guidelines for which biases are most likely to dominate for different personalities. Not every bias needs to be identified and managed for every investor. Some biases and heuristics may be more dangerous to the wealth of the investor, and with the help of Pompian's article, finance professionals will be better able to differentiate between what is important and what is not.

Risk profiles are typically identified with the help of a profiling questionnaire. As Professor John E. Grable demonstrates in the third part of the series, these questionnaires are often woefully inadequate for the task at hand. He focuses on two key metrics to evaluate whether a questionnaire is a good one (or, alternatively, to build a good questionnaire in the first place). *Validity* measures whether a questionnaire really measures what it is supposed to measure. All too often we encounter risk-profiling questionnaires that pretend to measure risk tolerance when they, in fact, measure risk capacity, or vice versa. *Reliability* describes the impact measurement errors might have on the evaluation of an individual. In order to be a viable tool, a questionnaire must be both valid and reliable.

No matter how good a questionnaire is, practitioners should always be aware that in the "heat of the moment," clients tend to deviate from their previously established risk profile. How circumstances influence risk profiles and investment decisions is the focus of the fourth part of our series, written by Elke U. Weber and myself. In this article, readers will learn that some dimensions of a client's risk profile remain the same regardless of circumstances, whereas the interpretation of the riskiness of stocks or bonds may change. This change, in turn, seemingly leads to changes in risk preferences, and practitioners can learn how to moderate these effects to the benefit of their clients.

Finally, the fifth part of the series, by Greg B. Davies, provides a look into the future of risk profiling. The main thrust of his argument is that the current practice of risk profiling focuses too much on identifying quantifiable parts of an individual's risk profile. In these efforts, advisers often focus on the short-term emotional reactions of an investor instead of on managing his emotions to keep him on track for long-term success. Similarly, advisers often focus solely on financial wealth rather than the whole set of personal circumstances. In his article, Davies thus opens the gate to full-scale financial planning and its benefits for individual investors.

Photo credit: Bloomberg/Getty Images

Though extensive, the list of topics covered in this series of briefs is by no means exhaustive. Risk profiling is a complex issue, but we hope that with the help of this series, advisers will be better able to assess the emotional needs of their clients and acquire a set of practical capabilities to better serve them.

Joachim Klement, CFA

INVESTOR RISK PROFILING: AN OVERVIEW

Joachim Klement, CFA

SUMMARY

In this discussion of investor risk profiling, current risk-profiling practice is reviewed and contrasted with regulatory demands and recent research findings. The current standard process of risk profiling through questionnaires is found to be highly unreliable and typically explains less than 15% of the variation in risky assets between investors. The cause is primarily the design of the questionnaires, which focus on socioeconomic variables and hypothetical scenarios to elicit the investor's behavior.

Existing research in risk profiling shows, however, that several different factors can provide more accurate and reliable insight into the risk profiles of investors. Among these factors are the lifetime experiences of the investor and the financial decisions the investor has made in the past. Another important factor is the influence of family, friends, and advisers. These factors can be identified and used by practitioners to enhance their understanding of client preferences and inform their recommendations of investment strategies and products.

INTRODUCTION

Investor risk profiling is at the heart of private wealth management. In theory, without proper knowledge of the investor's goals, time horizon, liquidity needs, and risk aversion, it is impossible to recommend suitable investments or build efficient long-term investment strategies for that investor. Even worse, if an adviser is not aware of the investor's risk profile, chances are the investor will buy products that help the adviser sleep well at night rather than the other way around.

To help ensure that consumers are sold only products that are suitable for them, every major developed financial market has instituted suitability rules. In the European Union, Article 25 of the Markets in Financial Instruments Directive II (MiFID II) provides guidance on suitability; in the United States, Rule 2111 of the Financial Industry Regulatory Authority (FINRA) deals with this issue.

Despite the central role of risk profiling in current investor-servicing processes, what constitutes an adequate, accurate risk profile—and a suitable investment based on it—remains an open question. Practitioners, regulators, and academics agree that suitability depends primarily on the characteristics of the investor, not the product itself (Davies and Brooks 2014).

Typically, practitioners and regulators use "risk profile" as a blanket term to describe the various facts and investor traits that need to be taken into account to identify suitable investments for an investor. Of course, the devil is in the details, because exactly which facts and traits determine the risk profile of an investor is a matter of opinion, and current research does not give a definitive answer. Moreover, findings from behavioral research fundamentally challenge some of the assumptions that current practice and suitability regulations are based on.

WHAT IS A RISK PROFILE?

Apple founder Steve Jobs, when asked in a mid-career interview about the reasons for his success, presciently answered that almost no one in business really asks why things are done the way that they are (Gau, Segaller, and Sen 2012). In this vein, this discussion begins with two fundamental questions. First, what is an investor risk profile currently understood to be? Second, what are the most common risk-profiling techniques used by practitioners?

Traditional finance uses the concepts of classical decision making, modern portfolio theory, and the capital asset pricing model (CAPM) to define the risk profile of an investor. In this model, investors are inherently risk averse and take on additional risk only if they judge that higher anticipated returns will compensate them for it. One of the fundamental results of modern portfolio theory is that, under the assumptions of the CAPM (Sharpe 1964), all investors invest in a combination of the risk-free asset and the market portfolio. The allocation of funds between the risk-free asset and the risky market portfolio is determined only by the risk aversion of the investor. Thus, in the world described by this traditional model, the investor's risk profile is given by the risk aversion factor in the utility function of the investor.

In reality, investors face constraints and do not act according to the model of rationality used in traditional finance (see, for example, Kahnemann 2012). A useful approach to dealing with these practical challenges is to distinguish between *risk capacity* and *risk aversion*.

Risk capacity applies to the objective ability of an investor to take on financial risk. Capacity depends on objective economic circumstances, such as the investor's investment horizon, liquidity needs, income, and wealth, as well as tax rates and other factors. The primary distinguishing feature of risk capacity is that it is relatively immune to psychological distortion or subjective perception. *Risk aversion,* however, may be understood as the combination of psychological traits and emotional responses that determine the investor's *willingness* to take on financial risk and the degree of psychological or emotional pain the investor experiences when faced with financial loss. These emotional factors are often even more important for practitioners to understand than the objective economic circumstances of the investor; yet, they are harder to measure.

Behavioral finance research has uncovered many systematic departures in investor decision making from the ideal of rationality used in traditional finance. For example, investors tend to exhibit loss aversion, insofar as the gain in utility from an increase in wealth is smaller in absolute value than the loss in utility from an equally large decrease in wealth. Although these systematic deviations from rational behavior have been widely documented, the challenge for practitioners is to identify to what degree a given investor deviates from idealized rational behavior, when the person does so, and—perhaps most consequentially—whether the practitioner can assist the investor toward optimal investment outcomes.

The combination of risk capacity and risk aversion constitutes what the finance industry calls the investor "risk profile." Investments are deemed suitable for the investor only if the investments' risks fall within the limits of the individual's risk capacity *and* risk aversion. Unfortunately, we as yet have no generally accepted list of objective economic circumstances that define risk capacity and even less, a list of psychological traits that define risk aversion.

Nevertheless, regulators require investment firms to establish investor risk profiles before recommending any financial products or investments for those investors. The rationale is that the "buyer beware" philosophy has hurt too many investors in the past. The prevailing regulatory desire is to put at least minimal investor protections in place. Current regulations reflect the complexity surrounding risk profiling, with many generally vague as to what factors influence a risk profile. Current regulatory guidance also differs among countries.

Article 25 of the MiFID II states,

> When providing investment advice or portfolio management, the investment firm shall obtain the necessary information regarding the client's . . . knowledge and experience in the investment field relevant to the specific

> type of product, that person's financial situation including his ability to bear losses, and his investment objectives including his risk tolerance.

In the United States, FINRA Rule 2111 states,

> A customer's investment profile includes, but is not limited to, the customer's age, other investments, financial situation and needs, tax status, investment objectives, investment experience, investment time horizon, liquidity needs, risk tolerance, and any other information the customer may disclose to the member or associated person in connection with such recommendation.

Risk tolerance features prominently in both regulations, but neither one says how to measure it or how it influences the range of suitable investments. The list of financial circumstances influencing the investor's risk profile is lengthy in the case of the FINRA regulation but not defined at all in the European regulation. The European regulation requires assessment of the experience and knowledge of the investor in the relevant investment field, whereas US regulations demand only an assessment of the general investment experience of the investor. It is fair to say that the lack of clear, consistent guidance by regulators leaves practitioners hanging in midair. They must ensure compliance yet lack clarity on what constitutes compliance. They also do not know what kind of risk profiling actually leads to investor protection and acceptable outcomes for the practitioner.

The result is a myriad of approaches to risk profiling and little evidence that these techniques meet any of their intended functions.

CURRENT PRACTICE

The typical investor risk-profiling process is shown in **Figure 1**. The task usually begins with definition and discussion of the investor's situation and the goal(s) that are to be achieved by the investments or portfolio. Serious issues arise at this point: Investors may have multiple goals, they may never have considered or articulated their objectives in this way, and they are not necessarily able to capture goals in terms of quantity or time. A common multiple-goal situation is posed by an investor who wants to save for retirement, which she expects in 10 years, while also wanting to save for a down payment on a new house. To complicate the situation further, she may also want to put aside a pool of liquid assets (emergency funds) that enable her to sleep well at night. What financial investment will achieve this last goal may be hard to define.

FIGURE 1. STANDARD PROCESS FOR RISK PROFILING

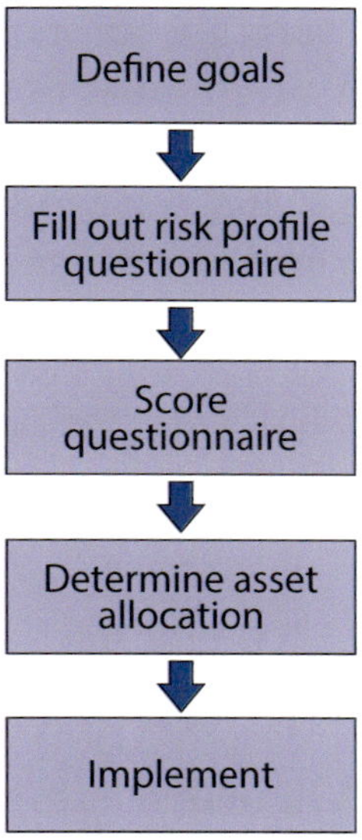

If we assume for the moment that the goals of the investor can be adequately defined, the process moves to filling out a questionnaire intended to quantify and document the risk aversion and risk capacity of the investor. At this stage, problems mushroom: In theory, to provide meaningful and reliable results, questionnaires need to be properly validated and tested. Validation and testing, however, are apparently seldom done.

Rice (2005) analyzed 131 questionnaires from investment firms and advisers in the United States, and his findings are troubling, to say the least. The number of questions used in the questionnaires ranged from 1 to 49. Probably the most troublesome finding is that 11% of the questionnaires he analyzed explicitly asked the investor to select a specific risk profile or portfolio. One has to wonder what use a questionnaire is if it asks the investor to provide the result of the risk-profiling analysis.

Even for more sophisticated questionnaires, however, the design is hardly robust. Although 65% of questionnaires had at least one question about the investor's time horizon, 35% did not ask about the time horizon at all. Some 70% of questionnaires asked about the investor's anticipated behavior in various market circumstances, but the treatment was superficial and never related to the investor's own financial situation. Yet, putting a scenario into a context relevant for the individual investor is important; a financial loss of $10,000 might be devastating to a student but not relevant to a millionaire. To truly assess the emotional reaction that a financial loss might trigger, the size of the loss has to be meaningful to the investor, and to evoke an emotional response, it has to be made relevant.

The influence of *framing* on the outcome of financial decisions has long been established (Tversky and Kahnemann 1981). Thus, hypothetical scenarios in questionnaires should be framed in meaningful ways for an individual investor—something that is hard to accomplish in paper-based questionnaires. To demonstrate the impact of framing on the outcome of risk-profiling questionnaires, I recruited 489 individuals through Amazon's MTurk service. Each individual was randomly assigned to one of three simple risk questionnaires for which they had to answer a few personal questions—age, gender, income, and education—as well as four scenario questions of the following form:

- **Version 1:** Assume you invest half your savings in stock A. After one month, the investment has *declined by 10%.* What do you do? Buy some more, do nothing, or sell?
- **Version 2:** Assume you invest $100 into stock A. After one month, the investment has *declined by $10.* What do you do? Buy some more, do nothing, or sell?
- **Version 3:** Assume you invest $10 million into stock A. After one month, the investment has *declined by $1 million.* What do you do? Buy some more, do nothing, or sell?

Questions were asked for a decline of 10%, 30%, and 50% as well as an increase of 10% in the stock price. **Figure 2** shows the percentage of respondents who chose to sell their stock holdings depending on the amount lost or gained. The differences between the three versions of the questionnaire are statistically significant.

In a more thorough analysis, I estimated ordered logistic regressions to assess whether the decision to sell stocks or buy some more was indeed triggered by the different frames of representation.

When differences in age, gender, income, and education of the respondents were taken into account, the $1 million frame (Version 3 in the experiment) led to a significant increase in the propensity to sell and a decrease in the propensity to buy some more. The differences between the $100 frame (Version 2) and the percentage frame (Version 1) became no longer statistically significant when the differences in age, income, and so on, of the respondents were taken into account. For all the respondents in the experiment, a loss or gain of $1 million was a vast sum of money whereas $100 was typically a small amount.

When dealing with large stakes—even if it is just on paper—the emotional reaction to losses is bigger than when dealing with small sums or abstract sums, such as percentage losses. This increased emotional reaction increases loss aversion. The percentage of respondents choosing to sell in the $1 million frame is typically about one

FIGURE 2. PERCENTAGE OF INVESTORS WHO DECIDED TO SELL IN THE HYPOTHETICAL SCENARIOS

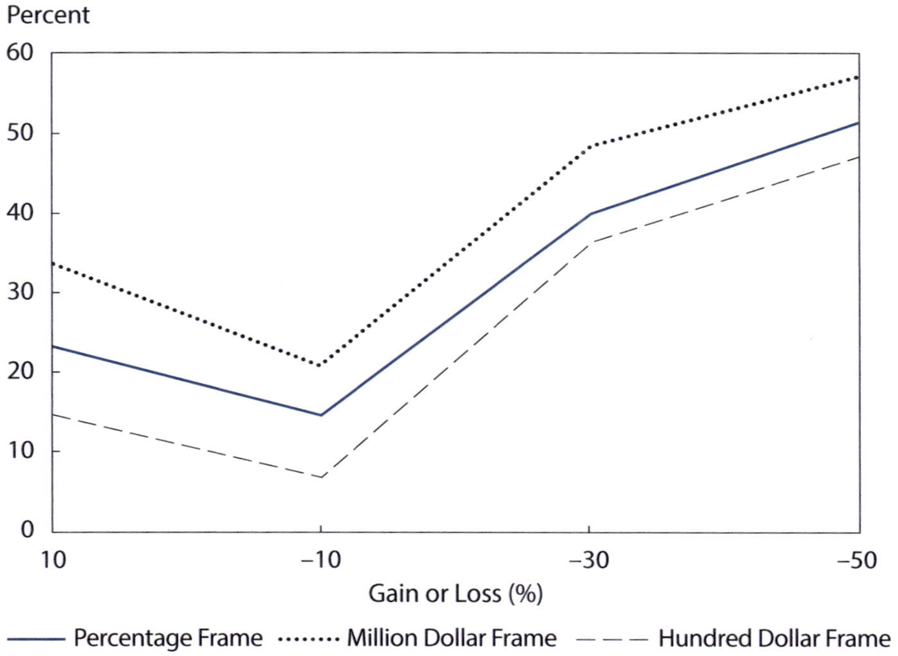

third higher than in the percentage frame. Unfortunately, the questionnaires analyzed by Rice (2005) all framed scenarios in terms of percentages or small money amounts. The current practice of risk questionnaires is thus likely underestimating the risk aversion of investors. When faced with a generic paper questionnaire, we might all be risk-loving investors, but when the next financial crisis hits, actual behavior might be very different from what we said we would do when answering a questionnaire.

> The current practice of risk questionnaires is thus likely underestimating the risk aversion of investors.

Once the questionnaire has been completed by the investor, the answers are then typically scored by the adviser/investment firm and matched with a specific asset allocation. In his survey of business practices, Rice (2005) found that scoring and mapping are done in highly subjective ways. Scoring was generally done on an equal-weight basis, even though some questions might have been clearly more important in determining the risk profile than others. Similarly, the confidence an investor had in specific answers was ignored in every instance, even though the abstract nature of the questions might lead to large variations in confidence levels. Finally, the determination of the resulting asset allocation seems to be typically done in such a way as to benefit the investment firm rather than the investor.

When all questions in the questionnaires surveyed by Rice (2005) were answered in the most conservative way, the allocation to equities ranged from 0% to 70%.

The influence of the adviser is greater than most investors (or regulators, for that matter) realize, as shown by Foerster, Linnainmaa, Melzer, and Previtero (2014) in an analysis of more than 180,000 Canadian brokerage accounts. They found that standard regressions that took into account risk tolerance (as indicated by answers to simple hypothetical questions), investor time horizon, financial knowledge, income, net worth, age, gender, and occupation could explain only 13.1% of the variation in the share of risky assets in investor portfolios. When the influence of the adviser was taken into account, the share of variation in risky assets that could be explained rose to 31.6%. In other words, the adviser turned out to be a more influential factor in the makeup of investor portfolios than the factors typically evaluated in a risk-profiling questionnaire. Similar results were obtained for the home bias in investor portfolios.

In summary, increasing evidence indicates that the current practice of using questionnaires to determine investor risk profiles is of limited reliability. The variation in risky assets in investor portfolios explained by variables such as age, gender, time horizon, and risk aversion is in the range of 5% to 15%, leaving the majority of the variation unexplained.

It is surprising that this lack of reliability has not attracted more attention by academics, regulators, or practitioners. But—to paraphrase Benny Hill—just because nobody complains doesn't mean that all parachutes are reliable. The number of complaints about the sale of unsuitable investments filed with the ombudsmen in Europe or the United States is staggering. The UK Financial Ombudsman Service recorded 2,079 complaints in relation to stock broking and portfolio management, with suitability questions being the main cause of problems (Financial Ombudsman Service 2014). The office of the Ombudsman at FINRA counted 1,283 complaints about allegedly unsuitable investments between January 2014 and November 2014 (FINRA 2014).

To be sure, the number of complaints is down from the years after the 2007–08 financial crisis, when complaints in the United Kingdom hit 2,474 and in the United States, hit an all-time high of 2,473 (FINRA 2011). Evidently, as long as the investments make money for the investors, suitability issues are not noticed or ignored. Once markets start to shake, the fragile foundations of investment advice as practiced today start to give way.

RECENT FINDINGS ABOUT TRUE INFLUENCES ON INVESTOR PORTFOLIOS

If the questions in the widely used approach of questionnaires do not explain the majority of variation in risky assets between investor portfolios, what factors *do* explain these differences? And can we use these factors to build more accurate risk profiles than questionnaires provide?

A growing body of research shows that the biggest impact on our risk preferences comes from our experiences and the environment we interact with (e.g., Klement and Miranda 2012). Basically, the factors influencing investor risk profiles can be placed in three categories:

1. Our genetic predisposition to take on financial risks.
2. The people we interact with and their influence on our views.
3. The circumstances we experience in our lifetimes—in particular, during the period psychologists call the formative years.

The risks we are genetically predisposed to take include financial risk. Although this fact is unsurprising, the *degree* of influence exerted by nature may be surprising. In a study of more than 37,000 identical and fraternal twins in Sweden, Barnea, Cronqvist, and Siegel (2010) investigated the pair's participation rate in stock markets and the shares of risky assets in the portfolios of the individual investors. (Sweden provides fertile hunting ground for research on the heritability of personal traits because the Swedish Twin Registry provides comprehensive data on all twins born in Sweden since 1886. In particular, the registry provides data on the rare cases when identical twins were adopted by two different sets of parents and reared in different environments.) Comparing the portfolio choices of identical twins and fraternal twins raised in the same household and comparing the portfolio choices of twins reared apart allowed the researchers to differentiate between environmental and genetic influences on risk preferences. Because Sweden also collects a lot of data on the individual portfolios of citizens for tax purposes, the researchers could combine the Swedish Twin Registry data with portfolio data from the Swedish Tax Agency to carry out a useful analysis of the risk preferences of a large pool of individual investors. Barnea et al. (2010) showed that 20%–40% of the variation in equities in investor portfolios could be explained by the individual's genetic predisposition to take on financial risk.

Similar results were found by an independent study of the pension fund investments of Swedish citizens by Cesarini, Johannesson, Lichtenstein, Sandewall, and Wallace (2010). Moreover, research has identified genomes that are linked to financial risk taking (Dreber, Apicella, Eisenberg, Garcia, and Zamore 2009; Kuhnen and Chiao 2009). Identifying a genetic predisposition to take financial risk is difficult for practitioners—even more so would be taking saliva samples to advise investors based on DNA. Practitioners may have some indirect ways, however, to examine the genetic predisposition to take or avoid risks, as discussed below.

Even if 20%–40% of the amount of financial risk investors take can be explained by genetic traits, the majority of variation is still unexplained. Here, the influences of our environment and the people we interact with come into play. As previously mentioned, the study by Foerster et al. (2014) showed that advisers have a bigger impact on the portfolios of investors than do measured risk aversion, age, income, and other variables. In addition, Hong, Kubik, and Stein (2004) found that the community we live in or the church we attend plays a similarly important role.

Another study confirmed the community effect; moving into a community with 10 percentage points higher stock market participation increases an individual's probability of stock ownership by about 4 percentage points (Brown, Ivkovic, Smith, and Weisbenner 2007).

Social interactions may also be at the heart of the cultural differences found in some studies. In a study of investors in 45 countries, Wang, Rieger, and Hens (2011) showed that the propensity to invest over time horizons of one month to one year differ significantly from country to country.

People living in countries that are less politically stable or that have a lower level of social cohesion, such as Russia, Romania, and Greece, generally showed a lower tendency to invest for the long term and a higher preference for quick gains. At the other end of the spectrum are citizens of Germany, Switzerland, and the Scandinavian countries, who showed a high propensity to invest for the long term. Such cultural differences may have many origins and correlate with many variables, but their influence is important and warrants study at a later time.

> **Life experiences are an important—if not the most important—contributor to financial risk preferences.**

Finally, life experiences are an important—if not the most important—contributor to financial risk preferences. In a groundbreaking study, Malmendier and Nagel (2011) showed that individuals who experienced the Great Depression during their early childhood displayed significantly different investment behavior from those who did not—even as many as 40 years later. Individuals who experienced the Great Depression were less likely to invest in the stock market and held, on average, a lower allocation to stocks than individuals who were born and raised in the relatively benign world after World War II. A study by Ehrmann and Tzamourani (2012) showed that the high-inflation period of the 1970s also had a lasting impact on investors.

Even 10 years after that inflation ended, investors who actively experienced the period were more concerned about inflation than younger investors who had not experienced that time.

A particularly important time for the formation of risk preferences is the period between ages 16 and 25. In this period, most individuals form their beliefs about the world, society, and life in general (Giuliano and Spilimbergo 2009). This period often coincides with, or just precedes, many people's first forays into investments. Thus, the experiences of individuals during this crucial time period influence their investment beliefs and their risk profiles for a long time. Giuliano and Spilimbergo showed that individuals who experienced at least one recession during their formative years exhibited political and economic views later in life that were different from those who did not. For example, these individuals were more prone to believe in the necessity of government intervention to redistribute wealth from the haves to the have-nots. Massa and Simonov (2011) investigated the interaction between financial risk taking and formative years' experiences directly by examining the investment portfolios of individuals during their university years. They found that when and where individuals attended college was highly influential on the portfolios they invested in.

The 2007–08 financial crisis provided researchers ample opportunity to study financial risk taking in real time. Emotions ran high during the crisis, and investors—and many advisers—experienced a disproportionate amount of stress. Thus, the financial crisis allowed researchers to investigate whether risk profiles are stable over time or whether, and if so, how, they are influenced by adverse market events. These studies found that risk profiles may well consist of a component that is stable over time and describes our general propensity to take on risk but also a variable component that is influenced by our emotions.

The "risk as feelings" effect (Loewenstein, Weber, Hsee, and Welch 2001) predicts that individuals make quick decisions about risks that are guided primarily by their emotions or intuition rather than rational considerations. Burns, Peters, and Slovic (2012) and Weber, Weber, and Nosic (2013) supported this hypothesis. Both studies used questionnaires to identify risk preferences and actual investment behavior throughout the financial crisis. The stable component of a risk profile seems to be the individual's assessment of his or her risk aversion; that is, the individual remains similarly risk averse throughout a stressful financial episode. What changes is the *perception of riskiness*. Once a decline has started, stock markets are perceived as riskier than they were, and only once they recover does the perception of riskiness decline. Thus, after a market downturn, investors are less willing to invest in stock markets than after a recovery or a prolonged bull market. How these perceptions of risk change over time and how the changing perceptions dynamically influence the risk profile demands further investigation at a later date.

PRACTICAL GUIDELINES FOR PRACTITIONERS

Practitioners need to be aware of these research findings, but perhaps more crucial is that they be able to identify the combination of traits and biases in each individual. Using generalizations based on the research cited here is not going to be helpful. It could, if a generalization may be allowed here, do more harm than good.

Psychometric testing is both an art and a science (which should be explored at a later time), but practitioners can use some simple techniques to identify individual traits more reliably than by using standardized questionnaires.

FINANCIAL *ANAMNESIS*

Doctors know that certain forms of cancer and other diseases have a significant genetic component. To identify patients who are at risk of contracting such diseases, they perform an *anamnesis* of the patient by asking for the medical history of not only the patient but also parents, siblings, and other relatives. Practitioners can engage in financial *anamnesis* to identify a systematic bias for or against financial risk taking by asking about the investment behavior of relatives. For example, studies show that children of entrepreneurs are more likely to become entrepreneurs themselves (e.g., Heaton and Lucas 2000). Similarly, stock market participation and other parental attitudes about the riskiness of stocks seem to correlate with attitudes of their children (Charles and Hurst 2003). So, asking about the financial habits of relatives can shed light on the risk profile of an individual.

INVESTMENT DIARIES

Of course, nothing conveys the truth more than the actual investment behavior of an investor. What an investor chooses to invest in and how the investor decides to buy or sell is more informative of risk attitudes than a questionnaire can be. Thus, advisers should investigate the past investment history of an individual. The ideal instrument to do this is an investment diary in which an investor records, in real time, transactions made and the reasons for the transactions. Over time, this investment diary paints a picture of the individual risk-taking traits of the investor. Few investors, however, systematically record their decisions in a diary, and few advisers encourage their clients to do so. In the absence of a diary, a collection of past transactions gleaned from bank statements can be informative. If the investor is willing to disclose past transactions and decisions to the adviser, these facts can paint a colorful and accurate investor risk profile. The danger of this method is that individual investors can learn from past mistakes and thus their attitudes toward risk may have changed over time.

INVESTMENT HISTORY BY MARKET ENVIRONMENT

Finally, advisers can shed light on the risk profile of investors by putting their investment history into the context of the markets. As discussed, the markets in an investor's formative years can leave a lasting imprint on the investor's risk profile. Investors who spent their formative years in the 1970s are likely to be more averse to bond investments and more prone to seek inflation protection than investors who spent their formative years in the 1990s. If an individual's first stock investments were made in the early 1980s or during the first decade of this century, the individual's attitude toward stocks might be very different from the attitude of someone who made his first investments during the bull market of the 1990s or in the last five years. Most investors today have never experienced a period of steadily rising interest rates and the impact of such a regime on investments. In short, the financial history of an investor might show the adviser where the investor might be overly sensitive to some risks or blind to some risks.

All of these tools—financial *anamnesis*, investment diaries, and investment histories—should prove useful to advisers in their regular interactions with clients.

Ideally, the results of the discussions would be documented, and with the help of these and other tools, the adviser can generate more reliable risk profiles in the future. We are only at the beginning of the development of such tools; unfortunately, the topic of how risk profiling can be improved in the future must wait for a later time.

SUMMARY AND OUTLOOK

Risk profiling forms the foundation of financial advice to investors all around the globe. Yet, the current practice of risk profiling via generic questionnaires provides a weak foundation for risk profiles. The questionnaires used at the moment are often not empirically validated and have little explanatory power. Regulators are increasingly aware of this problem and are requiring better tools. In its "Technical Advice to the Commission on MiFID II and MiFIR," the European Securities and Markets Authority states,

> Investment firms shall take reasonable steps to ensure that the information collected about their clients is reliable. This includes but is not limited to . . . undertaking valid and reliable assessments of their client's knowledge and experience and risk they are willing to take . . . and ensuring all tools employed in the suitability assessment process are appropriately designed for use with their clients and are fit-for-purpose. (ESMA 2014)

The crucial phrase in these sentences is "valid and reliable." Current practice does not conform to these standards.

These recommendations are not binding, but the report of ESMA was based on a thorough vetting process with stakeholders from the financial industry.

Moreover, these recommendations can be expected to be enacted into law within a few years. So, it is probably just a matter of time before advisers and investment firms in the European Union will have to comply with these standards. From the viewpoint of the end investor, such high standards can only be considered desirable, because they may reduce the risk of investments in unsuitable products.

Investment firms, for their part, could use these increased compliance demands to their advantage. By designing "valid and reliable" tools, firms can increase the trust their clients place in them and positively differentiate themselves from their competitors. By being an early adopter, an investment firm can demonstrate a clear understanding of why certain investment strategies or products may or may not be right for a particular client. The firm can thus use such tools to enhance the client's experience with the firm.

In addition, most investors do not like to fill out generic questionnaires, but few investors do not like to tell their story and talk about their past investment experiences. So, why bother with questionnaires? Of course part of the answer is that there will always be a need to document facts and data gathered from investors, but with the ideas presented here, hopefully investment firms and advisers can build a better foundation for their advice.

REFERENCES

Barnea, A., H. Cronqvist, and S. Siegel. 2010. "Nature or Nurture: What Determines Investor Behavior?" *Journal of Financial Economics*, vol. 98, no. 3: 583–604.

Brown, J.R., Z. Ivkovic, P.A. Smith, and S. Weisbenner. 2007. "Neighbors Matter: Causal Community Effects and Stock Market Participation." NBER Working Paper No. 13168.

Burns, W.J., E. Peters, and P. Slovic. 2012. "Risk Perception and the Economic Crisis: A Longitudinal Study of the Trajectory of Perceived Risk." *Risk Analysis*, vol. 32, no. 4: 659–677.

Cesarini, D., M. Johannesson, P. Lichtenstein, O. Sandewall, and B. Wallace. 2010. "Genetic Variation in Financial Decision Making." *Journal of Finance*, vol. 65, no. 5: 1725–1754.

Charles, K.K., and E. Hurst. 2003. "The Correlation of Wealth across Generations." *Journal of Political Economy*, vol. 111: 1155–1182.

Davies, G.B., and P. Brooks. 2014. "Risk Tolerance: Essential, Behavioural and Misunderstood." *Journal of Risk Management in Financial Institutions*, vol. 2: 110–113.

Dreber, A., C.L. Apicella, D.T.A. Eisenberg, J.R. Garcia, and R.S. Zamore. 2009. "The 7R Polymorphism in the Dopamine Receptor D4 Gene (DRD4) Is Associated with Financial Risk Taking in Men." *Evolution and Human Behavior*, vol. 30: 85–92.

Ehrmann, M., and P. Tzamourani. 2012. "Memories of High Inflation." *European Journal of Political Economy*, vol. 28, no. 2: 174–191.

ESMA. 2014. "ESMA's Technical Advice to the Commission on MiFID II and MiFIR." European Securities and Markets Authority (December).

Financial Ombudsman Service. 2014. "Annual Review of Consumer Complaints 2013/2014."

FINRA. 2011. "The Financial Industry Regulatory Authority's Dispute Resolution Activities."

FINRA. 2014. "Dispute Resolution Statistics": http://www.finra.org/ArbitrationAndMediation/FINRADisputeResolution/AdditionalResources/Statistics/.

Foerster, S., J.T. Linnainmaa, B.T. Melzer, and A. Previtero. 2014. "Retail Financial Advice: Does One Size Fit All?" NBER Working Paper No. 20712.

Gau, J., S. Segaller, and P. Sen. 2012. "Steve Jobs: The Lost Interview."

Giuliano, P., and A. Spilimbergo. 2009. "Growing Up in a Recession: Beliefs and the Macroeconomy." NBER Working Paper No. 15321.

Heaton, J., and D. Lucas. 2000. "Portfolio Choice and Asset Prices: The Importance of Entrepreneurial Risk." *Journal of Finance*, vol. 55: 1163–1198.

Hong, H., J.D. Kubik, and J.C. Stein. 2004. "Social Interaction and Stock-Market Participation." *Journal of Finance*, vol. 59, no. 1: 137–163.

Kahnemann, D. 2012. *Thinking, Fast and Slow*. Penguin.

Klement, J., and R.E. Miranda. 2012. "Kicking the Habit: How Experience Determines Financial Risk Preferences." *Journal of Wealth Management*, vol. 15, no. 2: 10–25.

Kuhnen, C.M., and J.Y. Chiao. 2009. "Genetic Determinants of Financial Risk Taking." *PLoS ONE*, vol. 4, no. 2.

Levitt, S.D., and J.A. List. 2007. "What Do Laboratory Experiments Measuring Social Preferences Reveal about the Real World?" *Journal of Economic Perspectives*, vol. 21, no. 2: 153–174.

Loewenstein, G.F., E.U. Weber, C.K. Hsee, and N. Welch. 2001. "Risk as Feelings." *Psychological Bulletin*, vol. 127, no. 2: 267–286.

Malmendier, U., and S. Nagel. 2011. "Depression Babies: Do Macroeconomic Experiences Affect Risk Taking?" *Quarterly Journal of Economics*, vol. 126, no. 1: 373–416.

Massa, M., and A. Simonov. 2011. "Is College a Focal Point of Investor Life?" *Review of Finance*, vol. 15, no. 4: 757–797.

Rice, D.F. 2005. "Variance in Risk Tolerance Measurement—Toward a Uniform Solution." PhD Thesis, Golden Gate University.

Sharpe, W.F. 1964. "Capital Asset Prices: A Theory of Market Equilibrium under Conditions of Risk." *Journal of Finance*, vol. 19: 425–442.

Tversky, A., and D. Kahnemann. 1981. "The Framing of Decisions and the Psychology of Choice." *Science*, vol. 211: 453–458.

Wang, M., M.O. Rieger, and T. Hens. 2011. "How Time Preferences Differ: Evidence from 45 Countries." *Norwegian School of Economics*, Discussion Paper 2011/18.

Weber, M., E.U. Weber, and A. Nosic. 2013. "Who Takes Risk When and Why?" *Review of Finance*, vol. 17, no. 3: 847–883.

RISK PROFILING THROUGH A BEHAVIORAL FINANCE LENS

Michael Pompian, CFA

SUMMARY

In the first piece in this series, "Investor Risk Profiling: An Overview," Joachim Klement set forth the challenges that traditional risk tolerance questionnaires present to advisers and their clients. He showed that the current standard process of risk profiling through questionnaires is highly unreliable and typically explains less than 15% of the variation in risky assets between investors. Klement explained that the cause of these deficiencies is primarily the design of the questionnaires, which focus on socioeconomic variables and hypothetical scenarios to elicit the investor's behavior. In contrast, research in risk profiling has shown that several other factors can provide more accurate and reliable insight into the risk profiles of investors.

Among these factors are (1) the investor's lifetime financial experiences (including the most recent period's return and volatility of markets), (2) the investor's past financial decisions, and (3) the influence of family, friends, and advisers. An additional factor, which is the subject of this article, is the psychological temperament of the individual investor; thus, risk tolerance is viewed through a behavioral finance lens in the article. With a better understanding of behavioral finance vis-à-vis risk taking, practitioners can enhance their understanding of client preferences and better inform their recommendations of investment strategies and products.

INTRODUCTION

We have seen a powerful recovery in asset prices in the wake of the global financial crisis (GFC). Lest we forget, however, more than $15 trillion in asset values evaporated in 2008–2009, wiping out gains earned in the bull markets of the 1990s and early 2000s. Clients were shell shocked, often frozen like deer in the headlights as to what to do. And just as history has shown, markets are cyclical and another bear market will occur again—it is just a matter of time. When times are good, as they have been for the past seven years, our skills as financial professionals can get dull because we have not had to deal with panicky, stressed-out clients. But it is crucial to "stay on top of our game" and keep our skills sharp. That is what this article is all about—staying sharp and doing the best possible job for our clients by incorporating behavioral finance into our practice. I have been doing so for over 15 years, and it has paid large dividends for me.

Understanding how investors make investment decisions is no longer a "nice-to-have" skill. In this new era of volatile markets, financial advisers must be able to diagnose irrational behaviors and advise their clients accordingly. Do you have trouble believing that? Consider that many top advisers across the globe are already applying behavioral finance to their practice. A number of years ago, I surveyed 290 sophisticated financial advisers[1] in 30 countries to ask them about their interest in and use of behavioral finance with respect to their clients: 93% of advisers surveyed reported that they were aware of key behavioral finance biases, and 94% were using behavioral finance principles with their clients. Some less experienced and quantitatively oriented advisers, however, are needlessly struggling with understanding their clients' behavior. Assessing risk tolerance is not just the client's job; it is also the adviser's job to interpret behavior and make adjustments accordingly. This article provides information that you, as an adviser, can use to help clients through the tricky business of managing their behavior to maximize the chances of attaining their long-term financial goals.

BEHAVIORAL FINANCE

Behavioral finance attempts to understand and explain *actual* investor behavior, in contrast to theorizing about investor behavior. It differs from traditional (or standard) finance, which is based on assumptions of how investors and markets *should* behave. Behavioral finance is about understanding how people make decisions, both individually and collectively. By understanding how investors and markets behave, it may be possible to modify or adapt to these behaviors in order to improve economic outcomes.

In other words, the way investors think and feel affects the way they behave when making investment decisions. Some of these behaviors are unconsciously influenced by past experiences and personal beliefs to the extent that even intelligent investors can deviate from logic and reason. These influences, which can be categorized and identified as behavioral biases, can affect the way risk is perceived and how risk is interpreted by someone trying to understand a person's risk tolerance. Later in this piece, I provide a framework that connects behavioral finance and risk tolerance; but before I do, I am going to provide an

[1]In order to be "eligible" to receive a survey invitation, advisers needed to have some kind of advanced professional or academic designation—an MBA, the CPA credential, the CFA designation, the CFP certification, or other significant professional accomplishment.

overview of how I classify biases. This overview is very important because the characterization of each bias is critical to understanding *how* to deal with it in practice.

In the first edition of my book *Behavioral Finance and Wealth Management*, I introduced a way of categorizing biases. The broadest category breakdown of biases is *cognitive* and *emotional*. Cognitive biases have to do with how people *think*. Emotional biases have to do with how people *feel*. In other words, cognitive errors result from memory and information-processing errors—that is, faulty reasoning. In contrast, emotional biases are the result of reasoning that is influenced by feelings. This distinction is critical. There are two types of cognitive biases: *belief perseverance* and *information-processing biases*. Belief perseverance biases concern people who have a hard time modifying their beliefs even when faced with information to the contrary. It is a very human reaction to feel mentally uncomfortable when new information contradicts information you hold to be true. For example, for decades many people have been under the false impression that eating sugar produces hyperactivity in children. Twenty years ago, several studies examined the effects of sugar on children's behavior. An analysis of the results of all these studies was published in the 22 November 1995 issue of the *Journal of the American Medical Association*. The researchers concluded that sugar in the diet does not affect children's behavior, but a very large number of people continue to believe that it does—an example of belief perseverance. Related biases include cognitive dissonance, conservatism, confirmation, representativeness, illusion of control, and hindsight.

Information-processing biases concern people who make errors in their thinking when processing information related to a financial decision. The simplest example is anchoring, in which people tend to estimate on the basis of an initial default number. If I asked you to estimate the population of Canada and remarked that I did not know whether it was higher or lower than 30 million, you would probably "anchor" your estimate around that number and adjust from there rather than make an independent estimate. Information-processing biases include anchoring and adjustment, mental accounting, framing, availability, self-attribution, outcome, and recency.

Emotional biases are based on feelings rather than facts. Emotions often overpower our thinking during times of stress. All of us have likely made irrational decisions in the course of our lives. Emotional biases include loss aversion, overconfidence, self-control, status quo, endowment, regret aversion, and affinity.

The distinction between cognitive and emotional biases is very important when assessing risk tolerance. With emotional biases, advisers often need to *adapt* to these client behaviors. It is hard to change the way people feel. With cognitive biases, however, we advisers have an opportunity to modify or change our clients' thinking—that is, to *moderate* clients' behaviors. About 15 years ago, I created a simple framework for applying behavioral finance in practice. This concept of identifying the various types of biases and indicating how an adviser can help clients overcome these biases can help *you* solve many of the most vexing challenges of client relationship management. To complete the thought, I also included level of wealth in this original concept. When you combine the two concepts, you have the diagram in **Figure 1**.

FIGURE 1. TYPE OF BIAS AND LEVEL OF WEALTH

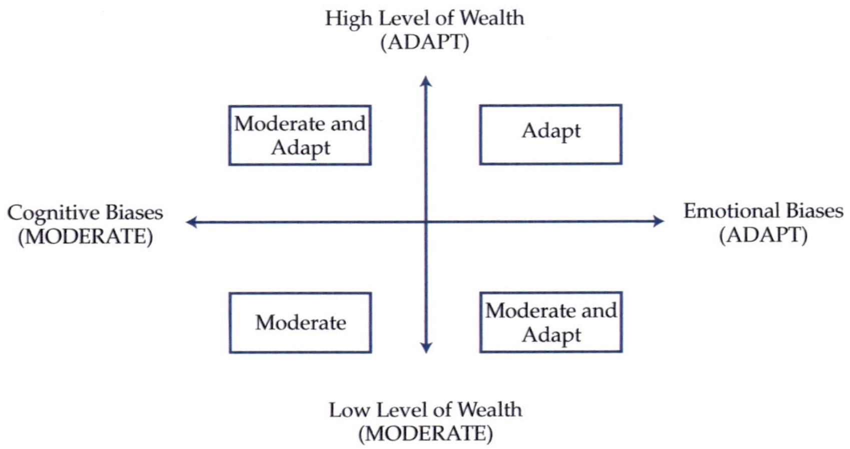

Later in the article, I connect these concepts to an overarching discussion about risk tolerance and how behavioral finance is inextricably linked to the risk tolerance discussion with clients. First, however, we need to define *risk*—not an easy thing to do, but the next section is a step in the right direction.

DEFINING RISK

Before we discuss assessing risk tolerance through a behavioral finance lens—which will involve looking at risk from the perspective of behavioral biases and ultimately investor types—we must first agree on what we mean by the term risk. Much has been written about the tension that exists between the *willingness* to take risk and the *ability* to take risk. For purposes of this article, *risk appetite* means the willingness to take risk and *risk capacity* means the ability to take risk. In the behavioral context, we need to further define risk appetite and risk capacity in terms of *known risks* and *unknown risks.* The reason is that, in general, when clients can at least understand and measure risks they are taking (i.e., *known* risks), they can accept the results. When the risks they believe they accepted include outcomes that are outside the bounds of what they expect or can reasonably understand (i.e., *unknown* risks), behavioral problems often begin. I delve into that subject in the next section; first, we need to further discuss the terms risk appetite and risk capacity.

Risk appetite is the amount of risk that one is willing to take in pursuit of reward. Risk appetite varies according to expected return; it may be expressed qualitatively and/or quantitatively. Investors with a high risk appetite focus on the potential for significant gains and are willing to accept higher possibility or severity of loss. Conversely, investors with a low risk appetite are risk averse and focus on stability and preservation of capital. Risk capacity can be thought of as the ability to absorb losses without having one's financial goals jeopardized.

The level of both risk appetite and risk capacity varies by individual; obviously, investors should not define their risk appetite without considering their risk capacity, but sometimes they do. In the end, risk capacity is the amount of risk a person can actually bear. On the one hand, an investor may have a high risk appetite but not have enough capacity to handle a risk's potential volatility or impact. On the other hand, risk capacity may be high but the investor, given his desire for risk reduction, may decide to adopt a lower risk appetite. Advisers can get a handle on these issues with their clients relatively easily when risks can be understood and measured—known risk. Risk has another dimension, however, that is not so easily measured and is often associated with irrational investor behavior—unknown risk. These two dimensions of risk are the subject of the next section.

KNOWN AND UNKNOWN RISK

Beyond risk appetite and risk capacity lies another important frontier of risk that affects clients' behavior dramatically: known risk and unknown risk—that is, those risks that can be reasonably modeled and understood and those that cannot. One of my favorite quotes of all time is by Donald Rumsfeld, US secretary of defense under President George W. Bush, who said, "There are known knowns. These are things we know that we know. There are known unknowns. That is to say, there are things that we know we do not know. But there are also unknown unknowns. There are things we don't know we don't know."

Often, people communicate that they have a certain risk appetite and risk capacity. But do the adviser and the client agree on what is meant by *risk*? How much known risk and how much unknown risk can the client handle? Known risk is what we might call "normal risk"—risk we can comprehend easily and quantify using historical data from observations of financial markets. And then there is unknown risk, or "abnormal risk," that occurs once every 10 or 20 years and falls outside expectations. We can think of normal risk as one or two standard deviations from the normal. We can think of unknown risk as three or more standard deviations from the normal. Although severe bear markets and crashes occur from time to time, it is probably best to think of 2008–2009 as an unknown or abnormal risk. At that time, the actual portfolio return fell outside the expected range of most models based on a normal distribution of returns.

When a decision is made on how much risk to take (risk appetite) or a measurement is taken of how much loss can be tolerated without jeopardizing financial goals (risk capacity), unknown risk can cause investors to behave irrationally. People must consider their likely reaction to known risk, and especially unknown risk, to get a complete picture of their risk tolerance. Combining all these concepts, we arrive at the equation for risk tolerance shown in **Figure 2**. Although beyond the scope of this article, risk tolerance questionnaires should attempt to elicit responses that identify how much known and unknown risk an investor can bear in *both* categories—risk appetite and risk capacity.

FIGURE 2. EQUATION FOR RISK TOLERANCE

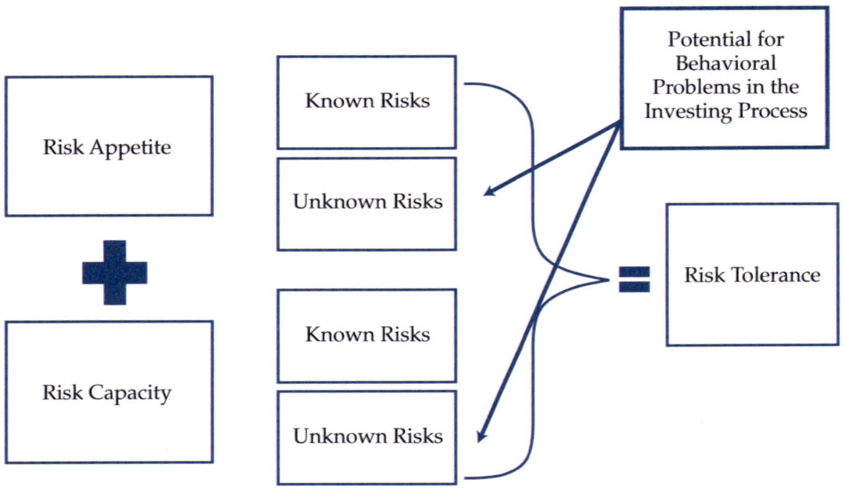

RISK TOLERANCE AND BEHAVIORAL FINANCE

Those of you who have taken the CFA exam recently or have read my books and articles over the years may be familiar with the concept of behavioral investor types (BITs). Identifying BITs through a process I developed called Behavioral Alpha® (BA) enhances the advisory process and allows advisers to work more effectively with their clients.

Although I am unable to review the entire BA process in this piece, I do review key elements of the process relating to risk tolerance. The BA approach is a multi-step diagnostic process that classifies clients as one of four investor types. Bias identification, which is done near the end of the process after the assessment of risk tolerance, is narrowed down by giving the adviser clues as to which biases a client is likely to have based on the client's risk tolerance.

BITs were designed to help advisers make rapid yet insightful assessments of what type of investor they are dealing with before recommending an investment plan. The benefit of ascertaining investor type at the outset of a relationship is an adviser can mitigate client behavioral surprises that might otherwise dispose a client to change his or her portfolio as a result of market turmoil. If an adviser can limit the number of traumatic episodes that inevitably occur throughout the advisory process by delivering smoother (or closer-to-expected) investment results—because the adviser tailored an investment plan to the client's behavioral makeup—a stronger client relationship is the result. For purposes of this piece, each BIT is characterized by a certain risk tolerance level and a primary type of bias—either cognitive (driven by faulty reasoning) or emotional (driven by impulses and/or feelings).

One of the most important concepts advisers should keep in mind is that the least risk-tolerant investors and the most risk-tolerant investors are driven by *emotional* biases, whereas the two types in between these two extremes are mainly affected by *cognitive* biases. To more fully appreciate how this happens and why, you may want to read my book *Behavioral Finance and Investor Types*. The key advisory concept, however, is that emotional clients tend to be more difficult to work with. Advisers who can recognize the type of client they are dealing with prior to making investment recommendations will be much better prepared to deal with irrational behavior when it arises. **Exhibit 1** summarizes each BIT's characteristics and behavioral biases.

GUIDELINES FOR PRACTITIONERS

As discussed in the last section, the least risk-tolerant BIT clients and the most risk-tolerant BIT clients are *emotionally* biased in their behavior. In the middle of the risk scale are BITs who are affected mainly by *cognitive* biases. This dynamic should make intuitive sense. Emotion drives the behavior of clients who have a high need for security (i.e., a low risk tolerance); they get emotional about losing money and are uneasy during times of stress or change. Similarly, highly aggressive investors are also emotionally driven people, who typically suffer from a high level of overconfidence and mistakenly believe they can control the outcomes of their investments. In between these two extremes are the investors who suffer mainly from cognitive biases and can benefit

EXHIBIT 1. RISK TOLERANCE AND TYPES OF BIASES

	Conservative BIT	Moderate BIT	Growth BIT	Aggressive BIT
Risk tolerance	Low	Medium	High	Very high
Bias types	Primarily emotional	Primarily cognitive	Primarily cognitive	Primarily emotional
Biases	Endowment	Regret	Conservatism	Overconfidence
	Loss aversion	Hindsight	Availability	Self-control
	Status quo	Framing	Confirmation	Affinity
	Anchoring	Cognitive dissonance	Representativeness	Illusion of control
	Mental accounting	Recency	Self-attribution	Outcome

from education and information about their biases by making better investment decisions. With aggressive clients, the best approach is to deal with their biases head-on and discuss how their investment decisions will affect such emotional issues as family members, their legacy, and their standard of living.

Clients who are emotional about their investing need to be advised differently from those who make mainly cognitive errors. When advising emotionally driven investors, advisers need to focus on how an investment program can affect important emotional issues like financial security, retirement, and the impact on future generations rather than focusing on portfolio details like standard deviations and Sharpe ratios. A quantitative approach is more effective with clients who are less emotional and tend to make cognitive errors. The goal is to build better long-term relationships with clients; BITs are designed to help in this effort. In the following subsections, I review four basic investor types: *conservative, moderate, growth,* and *aggressive.* The review includes the biases that are likely to be present with each type of client and some thoughts on how to advise each type of client.

CONSERVATIVE INVESTORS

CONSERVATIVE INVESTORS

Risk tolerance level: Low

Behavioral bias orientation: Emotional

BIT description: Conservative investors (CIs) place great emphasis on financial security and preserving wealth. Many have gained wealth through inheritance or by not risking their capital to build wealth (e.g., by working in a large company). Because they tend to be risk averse, CIs may be worriers; they obsess over short-term performance and are slow to make investment decisions because they are uncomfortable with change and uncertainty. This behavior is consistent with their approach to their professional lives—they are careful not to take excessive risks. Many CIs focus on taking care of family members and future generations, especially by funding such life-enhancing experiences as education and homeownership.

The biases of CIs tend to be emotional—endowment bias, loss aversion, and status quo—but CIs also exhibit anchoring and mental accounting, both of which also have cognitive aspects.

Loss Aversion Bias

Bias type: Emotional

Conservative investors tend to feel the pain of losses more than the pleasure of gains compared with other client types. Thus, these clients may hold only losing investments too long, even when they see no prospect of a turnaround. Loss aversion is a very common bias and is seen by large numbers of financial advisers.

Status Quo Bias

Bias type: Emotional

Conservative investors often like to keep their investments (and other parts of their life, for that matter) the same—that is, they maintain the status quo. These investors tell themselves that "things have always been this way" and thus feel safe keeping things the same.

Endowment Bias

Bias type: Emotional

Conservative investors, especially those who inherit wealth, tend to assign a greater value to an investment they already own (such as a piece of real estate or an inherited stock position) than to one they neither possess nor have the potential to acquire.

Anchoring Bias

Bias type: Cognitive/Emotional

Conservative investors are often influenced by purchase points or arbitrary price levels and tend to cling to such numbers when facing questions like, "Should I buy or sell this investment?" Suppose that the stock falls to $75 a share from a high of $100 five months ago. Frequently, a conservative client will resist selling until the price rebounds to at least $100/share.

Mental Accounting Bias

Bias type: Emotional/Cognitive

Conservative clients often treat various sums of money differently on the basis of where the sums are mentally categorized. For example, these investors segregate their assets into safe and risky "buckets." Although this behavior is usually not harmful, returns will almost certainly be suboptimal if all the assets are viewed as safe money.

Advice for Conservative Investors

After reviewing this subsection, readers might correctly conclude that CIs are difficult to advise because they are driven mainly by emotion. Although this conclusion is true, CIs are also greatly in need of good financial advice. Advisers should take the time to interpret the behavioral signs provided by CI clients. CIs need "big-picture" advice, and advisers should not dwell on such details as standard deviations and Sharpe ratios or else they will lose the client's attention. CIs need to understand how the portfolio they choose to create will deliver the desired results concerning such emotional issues as family members and future generations. Once they feel comfortable discussing these important emotional issues with their adviser and a bond of trust is established, they will take action. After a while, CIs are likely to become an adviser's best clients because they value greatly the adviser's professionalism, expertise, and objectivity in helping make the right investment decisions. In addition, CIs can usually benefit from the added risk that a competent adviser persuades them to take so long as the adviser carefully monitors the risk and does not allow it to become too large.

MODERATE INVESTORS

MODERATE INVESTORS

Risk tolerance level: Moderate

Behavioral bias orientation: Cognitive

BIT description: Moderate investors (MIs) often do not have their own ideas about investing but instead follow the lead of their friends and colleagues in making investment decisions. They are comfortable with being invested in the latest, most popular investments, often without regard to a long-term plan. One of the key challenges of working with MIs is that they often overestimate their risk tolerance. Advisers need to be careful not to suggest too many "hot" investment ideas—MIs will likely want to do all of them. Some do not like, or even fear, the task of investing, and many put off making investment decisions without professional advice; the result is that they maintain, often by default, high cash balances. MIs generally comply with professional advice when they get it, but they can sometimes be difficult because they do not enjoy, or have no aptitude for, the investment process.

The behavioral biases of MIs are mostly cognitive: recency, hindsight, regret aversion, framing, and cognitive dissonance.

Recency Bias

Bias type: Cognitive

Recency bias is a predisposition to recall and emphasize recent events and/or observations and to extrapolate patterns where none exist. Recency bias ran rampant during the bull market of 2003–2007, when many investors wrongly presumed that the stock market—particularly energy, housing, and international stocks—would continue to gain indefinitely. A similar mentality is emerging now that the more recent bull market of 2009–2015 has become entrenched in some investors' minds. Moderate investors may invest when prices are peaking, materially hurting long-term returns.

Hindsight Bias

Bias type: Cognitive

Moderate clients may be susceptible to hindsight bias, which occurs when an investor perceives past investment outcomes as if they had been predictable. An example of hindsight bias is the response by investors to the financial crisis of 2008. Initially, many viewed the housing market's performance from 2003 to 2007 as "normal" (i.e., not symptomatic of a bubble), only later saying, "Wasn't it obvious?" when the market had a meltdown in 2008. Hindsight bias gives investors a false sense of security when making investment decisions, emboldening them to take excessive risk without recognizing it as such.

Framing Bias

Bias type: Cognitive

Framing bias is the tendency of investors to respond to situations differently on the basis of the context in which a choice is presented (framed). The use of risk tolerance questionnaires provides a good example. Depending on how questions are asked, framing bias can cause investors to respond to risk tolerance questions in either an unduly risk-averse or an unduly risk-taking manner. For instance, when questions are worded in the "gain frame" (e.g., suppose an investment goes up), a risk-taking response is more likely. When questions are worded in the "loss frame" (e.g., suppose an investment goes down), risk-averse behavior is the likely response.

Cognitive Dissonance Bias

Bias type: Cognitive

In psychology, cognitions represent attitudes, emotions, beliefs, or values. When multiple cognitions intersect—for example, a person believes something is true only to find out it is not—people try to alleviate their discomfort by ignoring the truth and/or rationalizing their decisions. Investors who suffer from this bias may continue to invest in a security or fund they already own after it has gone down (i.e., they double down), even when they know they should be judging the new purchase objectively and independently of the existing holding. A common phrase for this concept is "throwing good money after bad."

Regret Aversion Bias

Bias type: Emotional

Moderate investors often avoid taking decisive actions because they fear that, in hindsight, whatever course they select will prove unwise. Regret aversion can cause moderate investors to be too timid in their investment choices because of losses they have suffered in the past.

Advice for Moderate Investors

Clients with the biases of MIs need to recognize that they tend to follow the lead of others and may not have their own ideas about investing. Not fully grasping their own risk tolerance, they may simply plow ahead with the task of investing. When an investment goes their way, they may convince themselves that they "knew it all along," a view that also increases future risk-taking behavior. Advisers need to handle MIs with care because they are likely to say yes to investment ideas that make sense to them regardless of whether the advice is in their best long-term interest. Advisers need to lead MIs to take a hard look at behavioral tendencies that may cause them to overestimate their risk tolerance. Because MI biases are mainly cognitive, educating MI clients on the benefits of portfolio diversification and sticking to a long-term plan is usually the best course of action. Advisers should challenge MI clients to be introspective and should provide data-backed substantiation for their recommendations. Offering information to MI clients in clear, unambiguous ways so they have the chance to "get it" is a good idea. If advisers take the time, this steady, educational approach will generate client loyalty and adherence to long-term investment plans.

GROWTH INVESTORS

GROWTH INVESTORS

Risk tolerance: Medium to high

Behavioral bias orientation: Cognitive

BIT description: Growth investors (GIs) are active investors with medium to high risk tolerance; some are strong-willed and independent thinkers. GIs are often self-assured and "trust their gut" when making decisions; when they do their own research, however, they may not be thorough enough with due diligence tasks. GIs sometimes make investments without consulting anyone. This behavior can be problematic because, owing to their independent mindsets, these clients maintain their views even when those views are no longer supportable (e.g., because of changed market conditions). GIs often enjoy investing and are comfortable taking risks, but they may resist following a financial plan. Of all the behavioral investor types, GIs are the most likely to be contrarian, which can sometimes benefit them. Some GIs are obsessed with trying to beat the market and may hold concentrated portfolios.

The behavioral biases of GIs are cognitive: conservatism, availability, confirmation, representativeness, and self-attribution.

Conservatism Bias

Bias type: Cognitive

Conservatism bias occurs when people cling to a prior view or forecast at the expense of acknowledging new information. GIs often exhibit this behavior. For example, assume that an investor purchases a security on the basis of knowledge about a forthcoming new-product announcement. The company then announces that it is experiencing problems bringing the product to market. GIs may cling to the initial, optimistic impression of the new-product announcement and fail to take action on the negative announcement.

Availability Bias

Bias type: Cognitive

Availability bias occurs when people estimate the probability of an outcome on the basis of how prevalent that outcome appears to be in their lives. People who exhibit this bias perceive easily recalled possibilities as being more likely than those prospects that are harder to imagine or difficult to comprehend. For example, suppose that GI investors are asked to identify the "best" mutual funds. Many of them would perform a Google search and, most likely, find funds from firms that engage in heavy advertising. Investors subject to availability bias are thus influenced to pick funds from such companies, despite the fact that some of the best-performing funds advertise very little, if at all (they do not need to).

Representativeness Bias

Bias type: Cognitive

Representativeness bias occurs as a result of a flawed perceptual framework when processing new information. To make new information easier to process, some investors project outcomes that resonate with their own pre-existing ideas. For example, a GI might view a particular stock as a value stock because it resembles an earlier value stock that was a successful investment, but the new investment is *not* a value stock. Suppose that a high-flying biotech stock with scant earnings or assets drops 25% after a negative product announcement. Some GIs might take this situation to be representative of a "value" stock because the stock is cheap. But biotech stocks do not typically have earnings, whereas traditional value stocks have had earnings in the past but are temporarily underperforming.

Self-Attribution (Self-Enhancing) Bias

Bias type: Cognitive

Self-attribution bias (or self-enhancing bias) refers to the tendency of people to ascribe their successes to their own innate talents and to blame failures on outside influences. For example, suppose that a GI invests in a particular stock that goes up in price. The investor believes it went up not because of such external factors as economic conditions or competitor failures (the most likely reasons for the price rise) but, rather, because of the GI's investment savvy. This behavior is classic self-enhancing bias.

Confirmation Bias

Bias type: Cognitive

Confirmation bias occurs when people observe, overvalue, or actively seek information that confirms their claims while ignoring or devaluing evidence that discounts their claims. Confirmation bias can cause investors to seek only information that confirms their beliefs about an investment and not to seek information that contradicts their beliefs. This behavior can leave investors in the dark regarding, for example, the imminent decline of a stock. GIs are often subject to this bias.

Advice for Growth Investors

GIs can be difficult clients to advise owing to their independent mindsets, but they are usually grounded enough to listen to sound advice when it is presented in a way that respects their independent views. As we have learned, GIs firmly believe in themselves and their decisions but can be blind to contrary thinking. As with MIs, education is essential to changing the behavior of GIs, whose biases are predominantly cognitive. A good approach is to have regular educational discussions during client meetings, in which the adviser does not point out unique or recent failures but, rather, educates clients and incorporates concepts that are appropriate for them. Because GI biases are mainly cognitive, educating GIs on the benefits of portfolio diversification and sticking to a long-term plan is usually the best course of action. Advisers should challenge GIs to reflect on how they make investment decisions and should provide data-backed substantiation for their recommendations. Offering information in clear, unambiguous ways is an effective approach. If advisers take the time, this steady, educational method should yield positive results.

AGGRESSIVE INVESTORS

AGGRESSIVE INVESTORS

Risk tolerance: High

Behavioral bias orientation: Emotional

BIT description: Aggressive investors (AIs) are the most aggressive BIT. These entrepreneurial clients are often the first generation in their family to create wealth. They are even more strong willed and confident than GIs. Very wealthy AIs have often been in control of the outcomes of their business activities and believe they can do the same with investing—they are overconfident. AIs often like to change their portfolios as market conditions change, which often creates a drag on investment performance. AIs are quick decision makers; they may chase higher-risk investments that their friends or associates are investing in. Some AIs do not believe in such basic investment principles as diversification and asset allocation; they are often "hands-on" and want to be involved in the investment decision making.

The behavioral biases of AIs are overconfidence, self-control, affinity, outcome, and illusion of control.

Overconfidence Bias

Bias type: Emotional (with cognitive aspects)

Overconfidence is best described as unwarranted faith in one's own thoughts and abilities—which contains both cognitive and emotional elements. Overconfidence manifests itself in investors' overestimation of the quality of their judgment. Many aggressive investors claim an above-average aptitude for selecting stocks; however, numerous studies have shown this claim to be a fallacy almost always. For example, a study done by researchers Odean and Barber[2] showed that after trading costs (but before taxes), the average investor underperformed the market by approximately 2% a year owing to the investor's unwarranted belief in his ability to assess the correct value of investment securities.

[2]Brad M. Barber and Terrance Odean, "Trading Is Hazardous to Your Wealth: The Common Stock Investment Performance of Individual Investors," *Journal of Finance*, vol. 55, no. 2 (April 2000): 773–806.

Self-Control Bias

Bias type: Emotional

Self-control bias is the tendency to consume today at the expense of saving for tomorrow. The primary concern for advisers is a client with high risk tolerance coupled with high spending. For example, suppose that you have an aggressive client who prefers aggressive investments and has high current spending needs—and suddenly the financial markets hit severe turbulence. To meet current expenses, the client may be forced to sell solid long-term investments that have been priced down owing to current market conditions.

Affinity Bias

Bias type: Emotional

Affinity bias, another emotional bias, refers to investors' tendency to make irrationally uneconomical consumer choices or investment decisions on the basis of how they believe a certain product or service will reflect their values. AIs are often subject to this bias.

Outcome Bias

Bias type: Cognitive

This bias occurs when investors focus on the outcome of a process rather than on the process used to attain the outcome. In the investment realm, this behavior consists of focusing on a return outcome without regard to the process used (i.e., the risk taken) to achieve the return. It is important for clients to understand how the outcome was achieved, not simply the outcome itself.

Illusion of Control Bias

Bias type: Cognitive

The illusion of control bias occurs when people believe that they can control or at least influence investment outcomes when, in fact, they cannot. Aggressive investors who are subject to this bias believe that the best way to manage an investment portfolio is to constantly adjust it. For example, trading-oriented investors, who accept high levels of risk, believe that they possess more control over the outcomes of their investments than they actually do because they are "pulling the trigger" on each decision.

Advice for Aggressive Investors

Aggressive investors are the most difficult clients to advise, particularly if they have experienced losses. Because they like to control, or at least get deeply involved in, the details of investment decision making, they tend to eschew advice that might keep their risk tolerance in check. And they are excited and optimistic that their investments will do well, even if that optimism is irrational. Some AIs need to be monitored for excessive spending, which, if out of control, can inhibit the performance of a long-term portfolio through withdrawals at inopportune times. In my view, the best approach to dealing with these clients is to *take control* of the situation. Advisers who let an aggressive client dictate the terms of the advisory engagement will always be at the mercy of the client's irrational decision making, and the result will likely be an unhappy client and an unhappy adviser. Advisers need to prove to the client that they can make great, objective, long-term decisions and that they can effectively communicate the results. Advisers who demonstrate the ability to take control of a situation will see their aggressive, emotionally charged clients fall into step and be better clients who are easier to advise.

CONCLUSION

In this piece, I have viewed risk tolerance through a behavioral finance lens while giving advisers some practical steps to follow when working with behaviorally biased clients who fall within the risk tolerance spectrum. There are two key takeaways:

- When viewing risk tolerance from a behavioral finance perspective, try to identify how your clients will react not only to known risks but also to unknown risks; unknown risks that come to pass are often the source of behavioral issues that can derail an investment plan.

- When advising clients, it is essential to distinguish between the various types of biases you encounter. If you are dealing with emotional biases, your advice should be tailored to that type of behavior; if you are dealing with cognitive biases, your advice should reflect that situation.

In an overarching sense, I suggest that you try to discuss these issues with your clients as often as possible. I know it is not always easy to discuss psychological issues during the investment process, but if you are successful, you will have very satisfied, long-term clients.

FINANCIAL RISK TOLERANCE: A PSYCHOMETRIC REVIEW

John E. Grable

INTRODUCTION AND SUMMARY

The concept of risk, and the specific evaluation of risk attitudes and risk taking, has a long and colorful history. Bernstein (1996) wrote the seminal review of the history of risk, pointing out that the concept of risk being related to outcome probabilities goes back more than 800 years. The first major breakthrough in thinking about risk, however, occurred in 1738 when Daniel Bernoulli used his knowledge of probabilities to uncover an important relationship between wealth and risk taking. He concluded that individuals prefer to take less risk and that they demand greater potential returns to engage in risky activities. Bernoulli's work laid the foundation for the development of expected utility theory and modern portfolio management principles. However, challenges to assumptions imbedded in the standard utility function began to emerge shortly after World War II. The notion that individuals, when dealing with financial decisions, always make rational choices across scenarios could not be fully supported empirically.

The first systematic risk attitude measurements were developed in the late 1950s. Kogan and Wallach (1964), for example, created the choice dilemma questionnaire, which remained a standard paradigm for the next 30 years. Their assessment tool was based on asking respondents to indicate the lowest probability of success required to undertake a risky choice in 12 scenarios dealing with a multitude of contexts. The data demonstrated that choice dilemmas did not do a consistently good job at explaining or predicting an individual's behavior (Kamalanabhan, Sunder, and Vasanthi 2000), particularly in the domain of investment and financial planning.

As behavioral economics and behavior finance gained traction as fields of study, researchers and investment professionals justifiably began to question both traditional models of economic behavior and the tools used to evaluate client attitudes. A general skepticism regarding existing frameworks led to the publication of a handful of validated financial risk-tolerance assessment instruments in the 1980s (MacCrimmon and Wehrung 1984; The American College 1994). Since that time, dozens (if not hundreds) of tools have emerged to evaluate an individual's willingness to engage in a financial behavior in which at least one outcome is both unknown and potentially negative. Nearly all of these instruments have been designed by practitioners and firms. Unfortunately, few risk-tolerance assessment tests have been created using recognized test theory principles.

This review provides financial analysts, investment professionals, and financial planners with an examination of how financial risk-tolerance tests can and should be evaluated. The review begins by clarifying terms related to risk taking. A broad overview of two important measurement terms, validity and reliability, follows. The review concludes with examples for practice.

DEFINITION OF TERMS

Financial risk tolerance is a ubiquitous phrase commonly used among financial advisers. When used broadly, financial risk tolerance is sometimes used as a catchall for many risk-related concepts. It is important to note, however, that financial risk tolerance has a very specific meaning. Cordell (2001) stated that financial risk tolerance is the maximum degree of uncertainty someone is willing to accept when making a financial decision that entails the possibility of a loss. This statement matches well with the International Organization for Standardization's (2006) definition that financial risk tolerance is the extent to which someone is willing to experience a less favorable outcome in the pursuit of an outcome with more favorable attributes. When framed this way, financial risk tolerance is distinct from concepts such as risk preference, risk perception, risk capacity, risk need, or risk composure. Each of these concepts is an essential input into the development of a person's risk profile; however, these terms are not interchangeable. **Exhibit 1** provides a brief summary of common risk terms. These definitions follow the nomenclature provided by Nobre and Grable (2015), who culled the literature for definitional frameworks.

EXHIBIT 1. RISK TERMS AND DEFINITIONS

Risk Term	Definition
Risk aversion	The inverse of risk tolerance.
Risk capacity	An objective evaluation of an individual's financial ability to withstand a financial loss.
Risk composure	An individual's propensity to behave in a consistent manner; sometimes called risk appetite (Carr 2014).
Risk need	The amount of risk an individual needs to take to reach a financial objective; typically based on a predetermined required rate of return.
Risk perception	A subjective evaluation, based on a cognitive appraisal, of the riskiness of a decision outcome.
Risk preference	An individual's general feeling that one situation is better than another.
Risk profile	An amalgamation of factors that help shape an individual's risk-taking behavior.
Risk tolerance	The willingness to engage in a risky behavior in which possible outcomes can be negative.

The following discussion summarizes issues related to the evaluation of risk tolerance specifically, and risk assessment generally.

THE SCIENCE OF PSYCHOMETRICS AND THE EVALUATION OF FINANCIAL RISK TOLERANCE

Psychometrics is a field of study that combines concepts from psychology and statistics into tools and techniques to improve psychological measurement. When psychologists, test developers, and test evaluators think about behavior, they tend to distinguish between intellectual (cognitive) and emotional (affective) pursuits. Some tests are designed to measure cognitive ability. Examples include US college-entrance examinations such as the SAT and ACT. Other tests focus on evaluating affective domains of behavior, such as personality characteristics and attitudes. Risk tolerance falls within this latter category. Generally, it is easier to measure cognitive, rather than affective, aspects of human behavior.

The application of scientific principles to the study of psychological states is a relatively new development. The origins of the field go back to the mid-1800s when researchers began to investigate intelligence from an evolutionary perspective. Since the 1930s, psychometrics has evolved dramatically. The field now encompasses the measurement and evaluation of personality, beliefs, achievement, and attitudes.

Initially, psychometricians were united around concepts embedded in what is now called classical test theory (CTT). As the field has matured, an approach known as item response theory (IRT) has been proposed as an alternative method of test evaluation. IRT had its start with tests measuring cognitive characteristics, but the principles have also been applied to tests measuring personality characteristics. The basic idea underlying IRT is that not all questions on a test measure a given characteristic to the same extent. For instance, on a cognitive test, not all questions are equally difficult. Some questions are answered correctly by everyone taking the test, whereas other questions are so hard that they can be answered correctly by only the most proficient test takers. Likewise, on personality tests, not all questions tap the measured characteristic equally. Thus, test questions can be assigned different weights based on how well they can differentiate between test takers with different levels of ability (or some other characteristic being measured). Different versions of IRT exist, based on the number of aspects of the test situation a researcher considers when developing and scoring the test. One-parameter models take into account only the test questions' difficulty. Two-parameter models take into consideration question difficulty, as well as the test taker's ability, whereas three-parameter models consider question difficulty, the test taker's ability, and the fact that guessing occurs on tests.

In a test created based on CTT, everyone takes the same test. In contrast, on a test developed using IRT, it is not necessary that all test takers be administered all the same questions. The questions individuals get asked depend on their skill level on a cognitive test (or level of a characteristic on an affective domain), as estimated by a set of questions administered at the beginning of the test. IRT proponents claim that this method allows for tailoring of test items to each test taker's ability level (adaptive testing). Another advantage of IRT is that different versions of a particular test can be equated more precisely for difficulty level. The chief disadvantage associated with IRT is that the statistical assumptions needed to use it correctly are more difficult to meet than with CTT, and typically a much larger sample size is needed to develop the test (relative to the sample size required in CTT).

Proponents of CTT and advocates of IRT do not agree about which method is superior for a given purpose. However, because nearly all financial risk-tolerance measures have been developed using CTT, the discussion in the remainder of this review is restricted to the CTT method of test design. Readers interested in a nonmathematical primer on IRT models should review DeMars (2010).

BASIC NOTIONS UNDERLYING CLASSICAL TEST THEORY

CTT is based on the notion that the score an individual obtains on a test is composed of two parts: a true score and measurement error. This relationship is expressed in the following formula:

Observed score = True score + Measurement error.

This true score represents an individual's correct score without contamination by any factors unrelated to the construct being assessed. However, it is impossible to totally avoid such contamination, and therefore, any given administration of a test is merely an estimate of this true score because each administration is tainted to at least some degree by measurement error. The true score can never be observed, only approximated.

If a test were to be administered thousands of times to the same individual, the scores that person obtained on each administration would vary, with the resultant scores typically being distributed in the form of the normal (bell-shaped) curve. The fewer the errors, the narrower the spread. Barring any change in the characteristic being measured, and no practice effects (not really possible), the observed differences in these scores on the same test would be caused by the amount of error in each score. Some scores would have little error, whereas other scores would have much error. Some scores would underestimate the person's true status on the characteristic of interest, whereas other scores would overestimate it. The average score across the multiple administrations would most closely approximate the true score because it counterbalances errors of underestimation and overestimation. Because it is not possible to obtain a true score, classical test theorists rely on observed scores to determine the quality of a measurement and to estimate the range within which the true score is likely to be.

The most important takeaway is that an observed score will begin to match the theoretical true score as measurement error decreases. All other things being equal, the less measurement error in the observed score, the better the test and the narrower the range in which the true score falls. Researchers will want to have as narrow a range as possible. In other words, the better a test is in practice, the less measurement error it will have and, therefore, the more precise estimates can be about the range in which the true score is likely to fall. Although overly simplified here, it follows that the quality of a test or other measurement tool, such as a risk-tolerance questionnaire, developed using CTT principles can be evaluated using two psychometric concepts: validity and reliability.

VALIDITY

Validity refers to the extent to which a measurement tool measures the attribute it was designed to evaluate. As noted by Roszkowski (2011), a test can be valid for one purpose yet invalid for another, which is particularly true for those who use risk-tolerance questionnaires. Some questionnaires are designed to measure an individual's willingness to engage in a risky financial behavior, whereas other tests are developed to gauge an individual's risk preference, risk perception, or risk capacity. Some evaluation scales are developed to provide a comprehensive measure of someone's risk profile. Thus, it is important to understand the purpose of an instrument and its intended audience before concluding that it is valid.

Generally, validity is measured using a combination of techniques. When an instrument is first developed, and as long as psychometric procedures are used, the test developer brings together several subject matter experts to identify preexisting questions and/or to write new questions. The use of experts to recommend and screen questions is the primary way *content validity* is ensured.

It is worth noting at this point that content validity shapes many of the outcomes associated with the use of a risk-tolerance questionnaire. An adviser who hopes to obtain a comprehensive risk profile for a client will likely be disappointed if he or she uses a questionnaire that was designed to measure the client's willingness to take risk in a specific context. Alternatively, an adviser who needs a specific evaluation score for a client's risk perceptions will find that a comprehensive risk-profiling questionnaire will provide an invalid output.

Construct validity is an important aspect of test development. Something that cannot easily be observed is considered a *construct*. Risk tolerance is a construct. A risk-tolerance test will have construct validity if the items that make up the test are actually related to the construct. A risk-tolerance questionnaire that includes questions related to a client's time horizon, cash flow needs, or economic expectations will have low construct validity. Why? These items, although important to know in their own right, are only tangentially associated with a client's willingness to engage in a risky financial behavior in which a loss is possible. A factor, such as a client's investment time horizon, may be a critical input into portfolio management decisions, but it is not theoretically associated with the construct of risk tolerance.

A subtype of construct validity is called *convergent* (*divergent*) *validity*. Scores on a test of a particular construct should be correlated with other tests of that same or a similar construct (convergent validity) but be unrelated (or related to a lesser degree) to scores from tests of dissimilar constructs (divergent validity). Convergent validity can be demonstrated by correlating scores from a newly developed test with scores from an established scale that is known to measure something closely associated with what the new test measures. For example, a reasonable assumption is that scores from a financial risk-tolerance questionnaire should be positively correlated, to some extent, with scores derived from a scale measuring sensation seeking (e.g., people who like to gamble are also likely to be more willing to take financial risks). Divergent validity exists when the scores from a test can be shown to be unrelated to scores from a test measuring a totally unrelated construct (e.g., scores from a test of financial risk tolerance should not be highly correlated with scores from a test intended to measure interest in gardening).

Of particular importance is the concept of *criterion-related validity*. This type of validity requires that the assessment instrument be positively correlated with a criterion, such as actual behavior. Two forms of criterion-related validity can be specified. *Concurrent validity* is assessed when test takers are asked about their behavior at about the same time that the test is being taken. Evidence of *predictive validity* is collected when a test is administered prior to the measurement of a behavior. Imagine, for example, that a financial adviser knows how a group of potential clients have allocated their assets among stocks, bonds, and cash. The adviser should expect a risk-tolerance questionnaire score to be logically consistent with each client's asset allocation framework. That is, in terms of concurrent validity, the evidence should show that clients with a high risk-tolerance score hold a significant percentage of their portfolios in equities. Predictive validity would be present if it turns out that prospective clients with low risk-tolerance scores sold equity holdings in the future during a market correction.

Criterion-related validity is typically measured with a correlation coefficient. Saad, Carter, Rothenberg, and Israelson (1999) recommended that the following correlation guidelines be used when evaluating criterion-related validity:

Above 0.35: Useful

0.21 to 0.35: Some usefulness

0.11 to 0.20: Acceptable in some circumstances

Below 0.11: Problematic

As an example, assume that a financial adviser uses a risk-tolerance questionnaire with 100 clients. If the adviser were to correlate risk scores with the ratio of equities-to-fixed-income securities or with future behavior (e.g., using 1 = sold stock in correction and 0 = held stock during correction), these coefficient guidelines could be used to determine the criterion-related validity of the questionnaire. For those familiar with statistical norms, these correlation coefficients may seem low. In terms of validity assessment, however, the size of the coefficients is acceptable. When explaining human behavior (such as investing), one variable (risk score) is unlikely to explain a significantly large percentage of the variance in the behavior. As such, modest correlation coefficients are to be expected and should not be dismissed.

When evaluating the validity of a risk-tolerance instrument, calculating sensitivity and specificity estimates is sometimes helpful. Imagine a risk-tolerance test that is designed to categorize clients into one of two categories: high or low risk tolerance. As **Exhibit 2** shows, four outcomes are possible: (1) true positive, (2) false positive, (3) false negative, and (4) true negative.

EXHIBIT 2. OUTCOMES ASSOCIATED WITH TEST ADMINISTRATION

	Actual High Risk Tolerance	**Actual Low Risk Tolerance**
High Risk Tolerance Prediction	True positive (TP)	False positive (FP)
Low Risk Tolerance Prediction	False negative (FN)	True negative (TN)

Sensitivity refers to how well a test correctly identifies the presence of an attribute. Sensitivity is calculated by dividing the number of true positives by the number of individuals with the attribute:

$$\text{Sensitivity} = \text{TP}/(\text{TP} + \text{TN}).$$

Specificity is the proportion of test takers without the attribute. It can be calculated by dividing the number of true negatives by the number of individuals without the attribute:

$$\text{Specificity} = \text{TN}/(\text{FN} + \text{TN}).$$

A test's *accuracy* is then the proportion of cases that are true to the total number of cases:

$$\text{Accuracy} = (\text{TP} + \text{TN})/(\text{TP} + \text{FP} + \text{FN} + \text{TN}).$$

Data from Exhibit 2 can also be used to predict the validity of a test at the individual level. Generally, a financial adviser will not know a prospective client's real risk tolerance. As such, the adviser will use a risk-tolerance questionnaire score to predict the client's attitude and behavior. A positive predictive value (PPV) refers to the probability that an individual possesses an attribute. A negative predictive value (NPV) describes the probability that the individual does not have the attribute. PPV and NPV can be calculated as follows:

$$PPV = TP/(TP + FP)$$

$$NPV = TN/(FN + TN).$$

For example, assume a financial risk-tolerance questionnaire was administered to 100 clients. After a market correction, the actual behavior of clients was assessed to see who held, added to, or reduced their equity holdings. **Exhibit 3** shows the results from the analysis.

EXHIBIT 3. TEST PREDICTIONS AND OUTCOMES

	Held or Added to Equities Holdings	Reduced Equity Holdings
High Risk Tolerance Prediction	40 TP	10 FP
Low Risk Tolerance Prediction	20 FN	30 TN

Each of the validity indicators can be calculated from data in Exhibit 3, as follows:

$$\text{Sensitivity} = 40/(40 + 20) = 67\%$$

$$\text{Specificity} = 30/(10 + 30) = 75\%$$

$$\text{Accuracy} = (40 + 30)/(40 + 10 + 20 + 30) = 70\%$$

$$PPV = 40/(40 + 10) = 80\%$$

$$NPV = 30/(20 + 30) = 60\%.$$

The risk-tolerance test has an overall accuracy level of 70%, with a slightly higher level of specificity. This degree of specificity means that the test does a somewhat better job of predicting the behavior of those with a low risk tolerance. In terms of predictive power, the PPV indicates that there is an 80% chance that those with a high risk-tolerance score will hold or increase their position in equities during a market correct or decrease their equity holdings if they have a low risk tolerance.

RELIABILITY

All risk-tolerance assessments contain some *measurement error*. The extent to which measurement error influences the calculation of a final score is important. A test's reliability helps answer the question of how much margin of error is provided by an assessment instrument.[1] Tests with high measurement error result in low reliability estimates. *Reliability*, within the context of financial risk-tolerance assessment, is an important concept because financial advisers almost always want to measure their clients' risk attitudes consistently.

Whereas validity indicates the extent to which an assessment tool measures what it purports to measure, reliability denotes how repeatable the score from an assessment tool is in practice. Consider again the traditional CTT formula:

Observed score = *True score* + *Measurement error.*

A reliability estimate indicates how much of the observed score is distorted by measurement error: the higher the reliability, the lower the measurement error (and vice versa). The higher the reliability, the greater the confidence that the observed score is closer to the true score.

Determinants of Reliability

What leads to measurement error? Random events certainly contribute to errors. The exam taker's mood or health situation can influence outcomes. Distractions in the room where an individual is taking an exam or environmental factors, such as an overly cold or hot testing room, can increase measurement error. For these reasons, nearly all standardized tests (e.g., SAT, Graduate Management Admission Test, Graduate Record Examinations, securities licensing exams) are administered in tightly controlled environments to minimize environmental factors that can increase measurement error.

The primary source of measurement error, however, comes from poorly designed tests with ambiguous wording, which explains the linkage between validity and reliability. Essentially, a valid test is generally a reliable test; however, a reliable test may not be valid. The first statement is self-evident. If the questions used to make up an assessment are badly worded, inconsistent, or confusing—signs of low validity—the resulting test will be less reliable. The second statement is more nuanced. A test may be very reliable, in that it consistently measures something in a repeatable manner, but it may not actually measure what it is intended to assess. For instance, some risk-tolerance tools used by financial advisers are thought to measure an individual's willingness to take risk when, in fact, the tests measure something entirely different, such as a client's investment time horizon, spending preferences, or some other personal characteristics.

[1] Within the psychometric community, reliability is the ratio of a test's true score to the observed score, based on the calculated score from the test.

Consider the following questions. Each question represents a typical item in what some financial advisory firms call an investment questionnaire, or more broadly, a financial risk assessment.

1. I plan to begin taking money from my portfolio in:

    a. 1 year or less
    b. 1 to 2 years
    c. 3 to 5 years
    d. 6 to 10 years
    e. 10 years or more

2. When you withdraw money from investments, you usually spend the distribution over what time period?

    a. 1 year or less
    b. 1 to 2 years
    c. 3 to 5 years
    d. 6 to 10 years
    e. 10 years or more

3. During the global financial crisis of 2007–2009, stocks lost 57% of their value from top to bottom. If you owned stocks that lost this amount in just a few months, you would:

    a. buy more of the investment.
    b. hold the investment and do nothing.
    c. sell a portion of the investment.
    d. sell all of the investment.

4. Which investment do you *prefer*?

    a. One with little or no fluctuation in value
    b. One with some fluctuation in value
    c. One with moderate fluctuations in value
    d. One with large fluctuations in value

5. You would invest in a stock or mutual fund based on a conversation with a coworker, friend, or family member.

    a. Strongly agree
    b. Agree
    c. Neither agree or disagree
    d. Disagree
    e. Strongly disagree

Which of these questions is an appropriate item to include is a financial risk-tolerance questionnaire? When answering, remember that risk tolerance is defined as an individual's willingness to take risk when a possible outcome is negative. It turns out that only one of the questions works reasonably well in this context. Roszkowski, Davey, and Grable (2005) noted that "mixing questions about more than one construct in a single brief questionnaire will almost invariably lead to an inaccurate assessment of all the constructs because none can be measured adequately due to the brevity of the questionnaire" (p. 68). Specifically, with these examples,

- The first question is intended to measure a client's investment time horizon.
- The second question is designed to evaluate a client's spending behavior.
- The third question—the best of the five examples—is intended to predict future behavior. Even though this is the best of the five questions, note that little academic evidence exists to suggest that people are particularly good at forecasting their future actions.
- The fourth question clearly measure's a client's risk preference, not tolerance.
- The fifth question is "double barreled," meaning that it requires a client to make one choice based on two conditions. Stocks and mutual funds are not exactly the same, which could cause confusion if a client's choice would change if stocks and mutual funds were presented separately. In addition, a client's answer might be different if the question asked about receiving information from one source, such as a family member only.

The sample questions illustrate how intertwined the concepts of validity and reliability are in practice. It is possible that these questions, when included in a questionnaire, might result in a high reliability estimate, even though the validity of the questions as risk-tolerance items is rather mixed. In other situations, these questions may work well. For example, if a financial adviser wanted to design a test to determine an asset allocation framework, these questions might be appropriate.

It is important to understand the primary determinant of a test's reliability: the number of questions. Generally, shorter tests have lower reliability coefficients. Thus, financial advisers should be skeptical of claims that one, two, or three questions can be used to adequately measure a person's risk tolerance. The *Spearman–Brown prophecy formula*[2]

[2] The Spearman–Brown prophecy formula was conceptualized in the mid-20th century. The formula allows a test user to estimate the reliability coefficient of a test when the number of assessment items is either increased or decreased. A practical example of the formula's use can be found in Beckman, Ghosh, Cook, Erwin, and Mandrekar (2004).

can be used to determine how many questions are needed to obtain a given reliability coefficient. Roszkowski and his coauthors (2005) used the Spearman–Brown prophecy formula to conclude that a 15-item risk-tolerance scale with a reliability estimate of 0.71 would need an additional 10 questions to achieve a reliability estimate equal to 0.80. This finding highlights a potential problem with the development and use of financial risk-tolerance tests. Ideally, a test should have a very high reliability estimate; however, this may require a large pool of questions. Unfortunately, clients cannot be expected to answer a battery of risk queries without becoming fatigued and bored, which helps explain why shorter assessments are preferred. When evaluating a test, a financial adviser should use professional judgment in balancing the number of items with an acceptable level of reliability. But be aware that for two tests of the same length, the one with the highest reliability coefficient is likely to provide the most consistent and repeatable outputs.

Reliability Scores

Reliability estimates are more difficult to calculate but easier to interpret compared with validity estimates. Within CTT, reliability is measured with a correlation coefficient. Correlations can theoretically range from −1.0 to +1.0. A test with a reliability of +1.0 is said to be perfectly reliable; that is, the same outcome is obtained when the test is given repeatedly. In practice, obtaining a reliability estimate of 1.0 is very rare (nearly impossible). In contrast, a published test would likely never exhibit a negative reliability coefficient. A negative coefficient would indicate that the test is seriously flawed.

Although a financial adviser can generally conduct a validity check on items in a risk-tolerance assessment, estimating a reliability coefficient directly is difficult. Instead, test users tend to rely on reported estimates from a test's authors or from an independent evaluation. The general rule is that whenever a test score is used to make judgments about an individual, the test's reliability should be relatively high. Nunnally (1967) provided guidelines on the acceptability of reliability estimates. The US Department of Labor revised Nunnally's original guidelines as follows (Saad et al. 1999):

Excellent = 0.90 or higher

Good = 0.80 to 0.89

Adequate = 0.70 to 0.79

Questionable = 0.69 or below

In practice, financial advisers should use risk-tolerance questionnaires with a reported reliability estimate of at least 0.70. Using a test with an undocumented reliability estimate or one with a lower reliability score will increase the probability that the obtained score varies too much from the theoretical true score. In other words, the likelihood that the observed score is accurate diminishes as the reliability estimate falls because there is too much "noise" (measurement error) to pick up the "signal" (true score) when reliability is low.

Reliability Measurement Approaches

Although it is possible for financial advisory firms to obtain reliability coefficients based on data obtained from their own clients, nearly all advisers instead rely on the estimates provided by the test publisher. A number of approaches to determining reliability are available to researchers. The most widely used method of reliability estimation is the *internal consistency* measurement. Reliability based on internal consistency is premised on the notion that the reliability of a test can be obtained by looking at the number of items in a test, their variances, and their covariances. A basic internal consistency approach involves taking a longer instrument, splitting it in half, and comparing the correlation of the two measures. This approach is called *split-half reliability*. Adjustments need to be made for test length to obtain an accurate estimate of reliability.

The problem with the split-half approach is that the size of the reliability coefficient depends on which items go into each half. An alternative internal consistency approach involves calculating *Cronbach's alpha* (α), which can be estimated as follows (see Cronbach 1951):

$$\alpha = (N \times \overline{C})/(\overline{V} + (N-1) \times \overline{C}),$$

where N is the number of items in the test, $\overline{C}$ is the average inter-item covariance among the items, and $\overline{V}$ is the average variance. Cronbach's alpha is conceptualized as the average of all possible split-half estimates of reliability. The value of Cronbach's alpha goes up as the number of items and their covariance increase. In other words, all else being equal, tests in which the items inter-correlate and the number of questions is large will produce high Cronbach's alphas.

Cronbach's alpha is used whenever the items in a test are coded as a continuous variable. An analogous test, the *Kuder–Richardson formula 20,* can be used to derive a similar reliability estimate when a test is composed of dichotomous items (Kuder and Richardson 1937). There is active debate within the psychometric community regarding the usefulness of reliability estimates based on Cronbach's alpha and the Kuder–Richardson formula 20; however, the general consensus is that tests that report reliability coefficients above 0.70 likely provide consistent and repeatable outputs for use in practice. Some statisticians warn that Cronbach's alpha assumes a true score equivalence (tau equivalent) model, which requires that a single latent trait (factor) underlies the scale, that the items forming it have equal variances, and that the covariances between these items must be the same (Tavakol and Dennick 2011). If these conditions are not met, Cronbach's alpha will underestimate reliability.

Other techniques used to measure reliability include test–retest reliability and inter-rater reliability. The *test–retest reliability* procedure involves administering a test to a group of participants, allowing a short interval to pass, and retesting the same group. The correlation between the first and second test provides an estimate of test reliability. Threats to this procedure include changes in environmental factors that can increase measurement error and *recall bias*, which is related to a test taker's ability to recall what he or she answered previously. *Inter-rater reliability* is used in situations where judges assign a score to a person or an object and the similarity among their ratings is assessed. For instance, assume that two investment professionals are rating the risk tolerance of the same group of clients based on an interview. Reliability would be high if they rated the clients similarly. A number of statistical measures have traditionally been used to measure inter-rater reliability, including traditional correlation coefficients (Pearson and Spearman), Cohen's kappa, and Kendall's coefficient (Gwet 2014).

VALIDITY AND RELIABILITY IN PRACTICE: THE STANDARD ERROR OF MEASUREMENT

Imagine that a financial adviser decides to do the maximum possible to assess and evaluate her clients' financial risk tolerance. After searching the marketplace, she chooses a risk assessment tool that provides an output based on a 0 to 100 scale, with higher scores representing a greater tolerance for financial risk. This financial adviser is so systematic that she decides to administer the test to clients on a yearly basis. After a few years, she starts to notice something that is both intriguing and potentially worrisome. Looking at one particular client, as an example, she notices that the risk-tolerance scores fluctuate up and down year by year. Over a five-year period, the scores are 75, 71, 82, 69, and 75. The financial adviser is concerned because although she knows that client scores can fluctuate, she did not expect such wide swings from year to year.

Should the financial adviser in this case be concerned? Fortunately, she can estimate whether the variation in scores exhibited by her client is within a reasonable *margin of error*. If she has used a valid assessment instrument (i.e., the questions are appropriate and the intent matches her purposes) and the average score on the test is 75, she can apply a standard error of measurement procedure to identify the range of scores where her client's true risk-tolerance score is located. To do so, she will need two pieces of data: (1) the reliability estimate for the test and (2) the standard deviation of the test based on a normed sample. Both of these data points generally come from the test's developers.

After completing her research, the financial adviser determined that the test's reliability is 0.65 with a sample score standard deviation of 10 points. With these data, she can determine whether the observed scores fall within the margin of error by applying the following analytic process:

Subtract the reliability coefficient from 1.0:

$$1.0 - 0.65 = 0.35.$$

Calculate the square root of the estimate:

$$\sqrt{0.35} = 0.5916.$$

Multiply the calculated square root by the test's standard deviation to estimate the *standard error of measurement* (SE_m):

$$0.5916 \times 10 = 5.9161, \text{ or } 6.0 \text{ rounded.}$$

Estimate a 95% *confidence interval* by multiplying the $\mathrm{SE_m}$ by 1.96 (this is the approximate Z-score associated with 95% coverage within a normal distribution):

$$6.0 \times 1.96 = 11.76, \text{ rounded to } 12.0.$$

The confidence interval can then be used to answer the financial adviser's primary question. She can use the average test score of 75 as the baseline, and add and subtract the confidence interval from the baseline. In other words, she can use the $\mathrm{SE_m}$ to identify that the client's true score falls plus or minus 12 points from the baseline or between 63 and 87, and that the variation in the client's scores, based on the test reliability and standard deviation, is reasonable.

However, $\mathrm{SE_m}$ may not be sufficient to directly answer the adviser's larger worry: Is a 12-point variation in risk-tolerance scores acceptable when the scores are used as an input to designing a portfolio recommendation or when drafting other financial planning recommendations? (When estimating repeatability, some psychometricians multiply the $\mathrm{SE_m}$ by a much higher [2.77] Z-score to obtain a 99% confidence interval;

this procedure provides an estimate of the expected variability—*reliability limits of agreement*—that one client may exhibit.) Although the answer depends on each client's situation, it may seem somewhat intuitive that this margin of error is a bit wide. It would be more beneficial to obtain an estimate in which the band of error is narrower. One way to move toward this outcome is to use a risk-tolerance assessment instrument with a higher reliability coefficient.

If, for example, the financial adviser could find a test with a similar standard deviation of normed scores and a reliability coefficient equal to 0.80, the confidence interval would fall to 9.0. The resulting narrower range in scores would give her greater confidence that the client's true score was somewhere between 66 and 84. The key takeaway is that the higher a test's reliability, the smaller the SE_m.

PRACTICAL GUIDELINES FOR PRACTITIONERS

The incorporation of financial risk-tolerance test scores into investment plans is a topic of interest to nearly all financial advisers. In the context of portfolio management, risk tolerance, as defined in this review, can be conceptualized in one of two ways. The first way is to view risk tolerance as a single input into a client's overall risk profile. Klement (2016) argued that risk tolerance is just one of several factors that comprise a client's risk profile. Other factors include age, investment objectives, time horizon, experience, and risk capacity. The combination of these factors, as evaluated by a financial adviser, determines the appropriate asset allocation mix. Carr (2014), for example, showed that a client's risk perception and risk need, in addition to risk tolerance, were the most important characteristics shaping an individual's risk profile.

The second way risk tolerance can be conceptualized is as a primary determinant of portfolio decisions. This matches the notion of financial risk tolerance as singularly more important within the context of investment management decisions than other factors, such as client financial knowledge. Nobre and Grable (2015), for example, noted that an individual's willingness to take financial risk is influenced by his or her risk perception, risk need, and risk profile—which they defined as being composed of risk capacity, risk preference, and risk composure. When viewed this way, a client may be willing to take risks when presented with one financial decision but be unwilling to take risks in another situation. This is true even if a client is both fiscally and emotionally primed to engage in either behavior. A client's perception that the risk in one scenario is lower (or higher) than in another may shape his or her willingness to take a risk. As shown in **Figure 1**, risk tolerance, from this perspective, acts as a mediator between a client's risk profile, risk perception, risk need, and engagement in a risky behavior. In this model, a client's time horizon serves to either enhance or reduce the influence of risk tolerance on behavior. For instance, someone with a long investment time horizon could reasonably be more aggressive than a similar person with a short investment time horizon.

FIGURE 1. FINANCIAL RISK TOLERANCE AS MEDIATOR

SUMMARY

Regardless of how one views financial risk tolerance within the investment planning process, several practical guidelines are worth noting when assessing and evaluating a client's willingness to take risk. First, the tool used to measure and evaluate a client's risk tolerance should be valid. Validity in this context means that the items reflect actual risk tolerance, not concepts related to time horizon, spending plans, or risk capacity. Second, the assessment tools should exhibit strong reliability. At a minimum, the questionnaire should have a Cronbach's alpha of at least 0.70. Third, and perhaps most important, the resulting score from a test should be used as a starting point in the investment planning process. As noted by Klement (2016), the derived financial risk-tolerance score (as well as the client's overall risk profile estimate) should form the foundation for ongoing discussions between the adviser and client. A valid and reliable financial risk-tolerance test is not only an essential investment planning tool but also an important data point that can be used to better understand a client's beliefs and behaviors.

REFERENCES

The American College. 1994. *Survey of Financial Risk Tolerance: User's Guide*. Bryn Mawr, PA: The American College.

Beckman, T.J., A.K. Ghosh, D.A. Cook, P.J. Erwin, and J.N. Mandrekar. 2004. "How Reliable Are Assessments of Clinical Teaching?" *Journal of General Internal Medicine*, vol. 19, no. 9: 971–977.

Bernstein, P.L. 1996. *Against the Gods: The Remarkable Story of Risk*. New York: Wiley.

Carr, N. 2014. "Reassessing the Assessment: Exploring the Factors That Contribute to Comprehensive Financial Risk Evaluation." Unpublished doctoral dissertation, Kansas State University.

Cordell, D.M. 2001. "RiskPACK: How to Evaluate Risk Tolerance." *Journal of Financial Planning*, vol. 14, no. 6: 36–40.

Cronbach, L.J. 1951. "Coefficient Alpha and the Internal Structure of Tests." *Psychometrika*, vol. 16, no. 3: 297–334.

DeMars, C. 2010. *Item Response Theory*. New York: Oxford University Press.

Gwet, K.L. 2014. *The Handbook of Inter-Rater Reliability* (4th ed.). Gaithersburg, MD: Advanced Analytics.

International Organization for Standardization. 2006. *Personal Financial Planning 22222:2005*. Geneva: ISO.

Kamalanabhan, T.J., D.L. Sunder, and M. Vasanthi. 2000. "An Evaluation of the Choice Dilemma Questionnaire as a Measure of Risk-Taking Propensity." *Social Behavior and Personality: An International Journal*, vol. 28, no. 2: 149–156.

Klement, J. 2016. *Investor Risk Profiling: An Overview*. Charlottesville, VA: CFA Institute Research Foundation.

Kogan, N., and M.A. Wallach. 1964. *Risk Taking: A Study in Cognition and Personality*. New York: Holt Rinehart & Winston.

Kuder, G.F., and M.W. Richardson 1937. "The Theory of the Estimation of Test Reliability." *Psychometrika*, vol. 2, no. 3: 151–160.

MacCrimmon, K.R., and D.A. Wehrung. 1984. "The Risk In-Basket." *Journal of Business*, vol. 57, no. 3: 367–387.

Nobre, L.H.N., and J.E. Grable. 2015. "The Role of Risk Profiles and Risk Tolerance in Shaping Client Investment Decisions." *Journal of Financial Service Professionals*, vol. 69, no. 3: 18–21.

Nunnally, J. 1967. *Psychometric Theory*. New York: McGraw-Hill.

Roszkowski, M.J. 2011. "Issues to Consider When Evaluating 'Tests.'" In *Financial Planning and Counseling Scales*. Edited by John E. Grable, Kristy L. Archuleta, and R. Roudi Nazarinia. New York: Springer.

Roszkowski, M.J., G. Davey, and J.E. Grable. 2005. "Insights from Psychology and Psychometrics on Measuring Risk Tolerance." *Journal of Financial Planning*, vol. 18, no. 4: 66–77.

Saad, S., G.W. Carter, M. Rothenberg, and E. Israelson. 1999. "Testing and Assessment: An Employer's Guide to Good Practices." Washington, DC: US Department of Labor Employment and Training Administration.

Tavakol, M., and R. Dennick. 2011. "Making Sense of Cronbach's Alpha." *International Journal of Medical Education,* vol. 2, no. 1: 53–55.

The author is indebted to Mike Roszkowski for his comments and his review of an earlier version of this manuscript.

RISK TOLERANCE AND CIRCUMSTANCES

Elke U. Weber
Joachim Klement, CFA

INTRODUCTION

The term *risk tolerance* is defined and used in different ways. Whether risk tolerance is a stable characteristic of a given investor or also takes into account external circumstances (e.g., economic shocks or the domain of the decision) depends on how it is defined and measured. This brief focuses on a definition of risk tolerance prevalent in the practitioner community—namely, an investor's willingness to take perceived risk (Davies 2017) or the trade-off an investor is willing to make between the perceived risk and expected return of different investment choices (Grable 2017). This definition derives from a psychological interpretation of the risk–return framework of classical portfolio theory (Markowitz 1952). It treats risk tolerance as an *attitude toward risk* and decouples this pure attitudinal variable from the *perceptions of risks and returns*—psychological variables in their own right and distinct from the expected value and variance of the distribution of possible outcomes (Weber and Milliman 1997).

Defined in this way, risk tolerance may differ among investors as a function of socioeconomic and biological differences but (with the exception of a brief boost during adolescence) shows stability across an investor's lifespan, financial shocks, and other circumstances. Risk tolerance, in this sense, is the mediator that translates perceptions of risk and situational needs and constraints into decision and action (e.g., Grable 2017, Figure 1).

The variables that change with market conditions and other circumstances are investors' perceptions of investment risks and expectations of return. In contrast to risk tolerance, which attaches to an individual and her biological makeup and personality, these variables change over time in response to changing external conditions. Therefore, an investor's risk-taking behavior (as revealed by her investment decisions) can look like it has changed, despite the stability in that person's risk tolerance. Perceived risks and expected returns are influenced by hopes and fears as much as by past returns and rational expectations and thus need to be assessed in their own right and possibly corrected.

A TALE OF TWO FRAMEWORKS

Apparent contradictions in conclusions about whether risk tolerance and risk taking are stable or depend on context give the casual observer the impression of a "confused landscape" (Davies 2017, 1). Such confusion stems in large part from the failure to differentiate between theory and conclusions about two very different species: *homo economicus* and *homo sapiens*—or, as Thaler (2015) more endearingly calls them, "econs" and "humans."

The consistency and stability of preference is a basic assumption in the framework economists use to predict rational behavior. *Homo economicus,* a mythical species that Herbert Simon compared to the gods, may have simple preferences, single-mindedly pursuing the maximization of material outcomes, but they apply these preferences systematically across contexts and integratively across their life cycle. High-level goals and decision processes used are assumed to be the same for every econ, although the utility of a given outcome and the importance of different dimensions (say, quality versus price) are allowed to vary. Time preference and risk preference are two parameters also allowed to differ between individuals, reflecting differences in values and acceptable trade-offs. In contrast to this allowed between-person difference, however, is an implicit assumption that a given investor's level of risk tolerance, defined as a parameter of the utility function that makes the investor risk seeking or risk averse in his choices under uncertainty, is stable across situations and describes that person in much the same way as a psychological trait does, invariant across circumstances.

This assumption of stable risk tolerance for a given individual is also reflected in regulatory requirements for financial advisers. In Europe, the Markets in Financial Instruments Directive (MiFID) requires financial advisers and financial institutions dealing with individual investors to understand and document the client's "preferences regarding risk taking, his risk profile, and the purpose of the investment" (European Parliament and European Council 2004 and 2006, Art. 35, 4). In its latest consultation paper on the subject, the European Securities and Markets Authority (ESMA) further specified that the questionnaires and tools used to elicit risk tolerance need to be "fit for purpose" and that objective criteria as well as a client's subjective biases should be explored (ESMA 2017). A client's risk profile has to be updated regularly to reflect changing financial circumstances, but the regulations make no mention of variable risk tolerance owing to changes in an investor's emotional or psychological state. But do humans, like econs, have stable risk tolerance that reflects a stable attitude toward risk? And if so, what accounts for observed instances of inconsistency in their risky investment decisions?

In addition to the *attitudinal* differences (toward risk and time delay) allowed for by economics, psychology allows for individual or situational differences in the *perception* of a situation. Weber, Weber, and Nosić (2013) demonstrated the importance of changes in the subjective perception of risk during the 2008–09 financial crisis. From September 2008 to June 2009, the authors surveyed a large number of clients of an online UK brokerage firm about their attitudes toward risk, their expectation for risk and return in the overall stock market, and the contents of their portfolios. The survey allowed the authors to measure risk preferences and perceptions in real time every three months during a period spanning the depths of the stock market crash of 2008 through the first months of the recovery in 2009. The results, discussed in greater detail later, show that risk taking changed substantially during the observation period. Changes in individual risk taking were driven mostly by changes in the perception of risk rather than changes in risk attitude, assessed directly as an attitudinal variable, which changed little over the time period that was studied.

As further described later, these results show that humans, unlike econs, use a wide variety of information and mental processes to make financial decisions. These mental processes include emotions; moral and professional rules of conduct, as well as other social norms; and, of course, rational calculations like those an econ, if one existed, might use. It is the emotional state of the individual investor that can change rapidly over time as circumstances change. Emotional responses are generally not "objectively reproducible": The same set of external circumstances might elicit very different emotions depending on the way these circumstances are "experienced" or processed by the individual.

Assume, for instance, an investor purchases shares of company A at $50 per share in July 2017. By the end of 2017, the share price has doubled to $100. The investor decides to keep the shares, and in June 2018, the share price is $75. Objectively, the investor has made a gain of $25 per share, but many investors might not feel too happy about this gain because they would consider it a loss of $25 per share since the beginning of the year. As Benartzi and Thaler (1995) have shown, investors tend to assess their investments in a relative fashion, comparing current value with recent values, and experience regret when share price declines relative to a recent anchor, such as the price at the end of the previous year. Compare this investor with another who made the same investment at the same time but did not know about the stock's value at the end of 2017. This second investor is still anchored to the original reference point of $50 rather than the year-end share price of $100. Her emotional state might thus be very different from, and happier than, that of the first investor.

This example can be expanded to ever-finer degrees of detail. The emotional reaction to an investment in stock A will depend not only on the price of stock A and its past performance but also on the investor's general mood when the information is presented to him, as a function of his personal experiences of sorrows and joys on that day. Even the day's weather (e.g., sunny or rainy) has been shown to influence investor emotions and decisions (Hirshleifer and Shumway 2003). Neuroscientist Lisa Feldman Barrett recently reviewed the evidence from neuroscience experiments, concluding that emotions in response to an event are highly dependent on the circumstances in which they are experienced. It is thus unlikely that two people presented with the same set of data—or even the same person at two different points in time—will have the same emotional reaction to it and make the same or even similar decisions (Feldman Barrett 2017).

Does all this mean that our efforts to define risk tolerance for individual investors are futile to begin with? We think not. The "risk as feelings" hypothesis (Loewenstein, Weber, Hsee, and Welch 2001) provides a theoretical foundation for the observed variability in risk taking and allows us to define and measure risk tolerance appropriately.

DISTINGUISHING BETWEEN PERCEIVED-RISK TOLERANCE AND APPARENT-RISK TOLERANCE

The previous examples of emotional reactions to changing circumstances notwithstanding, most of us know who among our friends, colleagues, or clients is more risk averse and who is more risk tolerant or even risk seeking. Some demographic variables influence risk tolerance and allow us to "cluster" our friends, colleagues, and clients into similar groups. Sahm (2008) finds that risk tolerance declines with age (when controlled for cohort effects) and varies with macroeconomic conditions (i.e., risk tolerance declines in recessions). Similarly, studies have documented statistically significant differences in risk tolerance between men and women, among members of different ethnic and racial backgrounds, and between married and unmarried persons, as well as among persons of different educational attainment.

If we want to understand which parts of risk tolerance are stable over time (and are thus somewhat like personality traits) and which parts change depending on the circumstances, it pays to take a closer look at the aforementioned study of UK brokerage clients (Weber et al. 2013). In a traditional modern portfolio framework, we would expect *homo economicus* to form a portfolio based on her utility function. This portfolio can vary from person to person but should depend on the expected return and volatility of the investment in question as well as the person's risk attitude. In this traditional model, risk attitude might differ from person to person but remain stable over time.

This traditional model developed by Markowitz (1952) can be generalized in a psychological model, in which risk taking depends on expected return, expected risk, and personal risk attitude (Weber and Milliman 1997; Weber and Johnson 2008). Note that in this psychological model, expected return and risk do not have to be measured by expected return and volatility as defined in a statistical way but can be expressed as the individual's subjective perception of expected return and risk. Changes in risk tolerance can then be the result of either changes in risk attitude or changes in the perceived risk or return of the investment.

In Weber et al. (2013), changes of perceived return, risk, and risk attitude were measured in real time during the height of the financial crisis. Every quarter, investors were asked to allocate a fund amounting to £100,000 into either the UK stock market or a hypothetical risk-free asset that paid an annual interest of 4%. Investors were free to allocate that money in any proportion to the two investments and knew that they could adjust their allocation in three months' time. Their allocation to the risky asset provides a measure of risk taking in a hypothetical portfolio. Additionally, the investors were asked to rate their risk attitude by providing their degree of agreement with three statements from the brokerage firm's own risk questionnaire:

- It is likely I would invest a significant sum in a high-risk investment.
- I am a financial risk taker.
- Even if I experienced a significant loss on an investment, I would still consider making risky investments.

These statements about risk attitude were complemented by subjective and numerical questions about the individuals' perceptions of the riskiness of the UK stock market and its expected returns. The subjective measure was a simple question about the prospects for the UK stock market's return outlook in the next three months (on a scale from "extremely bad" to "extremely good") and how risky the stock market would be in the next three months (on a scale from "not at all risky" to "extremely risky"). In the numerical assessment of the stock market, investors were asked to give a midpoint estimate of the market return they expected in the coming three months as well as estimates for the returns at the 5th and 95th percentile, enabling Weber et al. (2013) to calculate the volatility that investors expected the stock market to have.

Figure 1 shows the study's key result. Actual risk taking (the amount invested in the UK stock market) changed substantially throughout the financial crisis, dropping from an average of 56% to 46.5% in March 2009 before rising again as the stock market recovery continued throughout 2009. In contrast, risk attitude as elicited by the survey statements (and not shown in Figure 1) hardly changed at all throughout the financial crisis. What did change, however, were the subjective perceptions of market risk and market return. The UK stock market was perceived as substantially riskier in December 2008, after the Lehman Brothers collapse, and in March 2009, at the trough of the stock market. Subjective perception of market risk began to drop again only when the stock market started to recover in March 2009.

The subjective estimates of the return opportunities in the stock market were more stable and continued to increase as stock markets declined throughout the financial crisis. The change in the perception of stock market riskiness was the single most

FIGURE 1. CHANGES IN RISK TAKING AND SUBJECTIVELY PERCEIVED RISKINESS AND RETURN OF UK STOCK MARKET, SEPTEMBER 2008–JUNE 2009

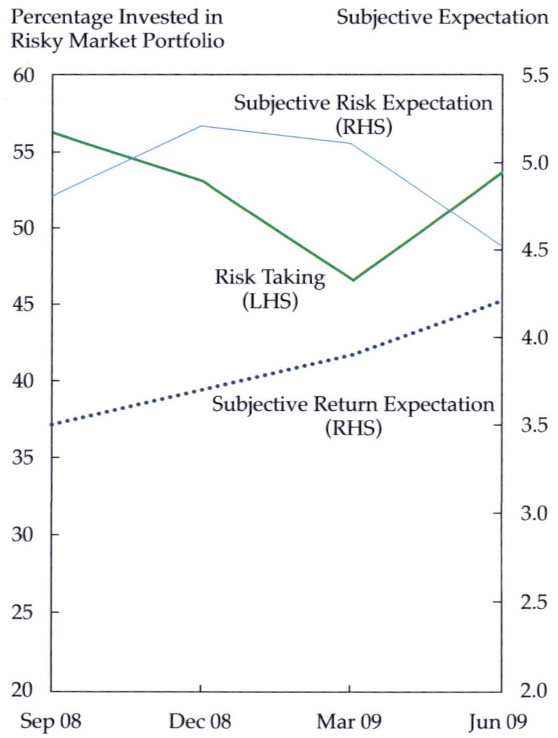

Source: Weber et al. (2013).

important driver of the change in risk taking. Note that this change in perceived riskiness of stocks is not necessarily based on numerical or rational expectations. Investors' numerical estimates of market risk increased after the Lehman Brothers collapse but stayed elevated and even increased toward the end of the study in June 2009. This trend indicates that perceived risk is an emotional concept for investors rather than just an exercise in rational thought and numerical analysis. It is this emotional reaction to financial markets that varies over time and drives risk taking.

Subsequent studies have found similar results. Nguyen, Gallery, and Newton (2017) confirm that Australian investors' investment decisions are influenced directly and indirectly by the perceived riskiness of financial markets. Hoffmann, Post, and Pennings (2015) show that subjective perception of risk and return influence trading decisions not only hypothetically via a survey but also in actual investor portfolios.

SYSTEMATIC DIFFERENCES IN RISK PERCEPTION

These studies bear both good news and bad news for financial advisers. The good news is that risk attitudes do not need to be assessed very frequently, because even during the worst financial crisis in decades, they remained rather stable. Risk attitude seems to be a stable psychological trait of an individual that can be assessed with the appropriate tools, such as a psychometric questionnaire (Grable 2016) or even a single general risk-attitude question that asks participants to assess their own willingness to take risks. There are also group-specific systematic differences in risk taking that may indicate differences in risk attitude, or in perceptions of risks or returns, that financial advisers should be aware of.

MEN TAKE MORE RISK THAN WOMEN BECAUSE THEY PERCEIVE THE RISKS TO BE LOWER

Probably the best-documented systematic difference in risk taking is gender based. Byrnes, Miller, and Schafer (1999) analyzed the results of 150 studies on the subject and found that, in most cases, men take systematically more risk than women. Their findings differed, however, among the domains in which risk taking was measured. Although there was hardly any gender-based difference in the propensity to use drugs or drink excessively, big differences between men and women appeared when asked about their behavior behind the wheel of a car. Reckless driving was far more prevalent in men than in women.

Weber, Blais, and Betz (2002) measured self-reported risk taking across different domains, ranging from financial decisions to social decisions. This study provides several important results.

First, and important for financial advisers to remember, risk taking differs from one domain of human activity to another. Just because an investor enjoys skydiving, for example, does not mean that he will also take on more risks in the investment domain.

Second, it is important to know why women appear to take on less risk in financial decisions than men. Some 560 undergraduate students of The Ohio State University answered 21 questions about financial risk taking on a five-point scale ranging from 1 (extremely unlikely to engage in risky behavior) to 5 (extremely likely to engage in risky activity). The average response for men was 3.49, and for women, 2.18. The main driver of these differences was not an innate difference in risk attitude between men and women. Instead, the variation in risk taking originated in a difference in risk perception. When taking on financial risk, investors have to assess three key variables: expected return, perceived riskiness of the investment, and the likelihood of different outcomes. When expected returns are higher or perceived to be higher, then we expect an investor to be more likely to engage in a risky financial investment.

Similarly, when perceived risks are higher, we expect investors to be less likely to engage in the investment. Weber, Blais, and Betz (2002) found that systematic differences in risk perception drove the differences in risk attitude. Women were, on average, more cautious because they perceived financial decisions to be riskier than men did. This increased perception of risk can be documented in every domain of risk taking except the social domain, where women have a lower risk perception than men, presumably because women have greater familiarity with risky decisions in this domain. Greater familiarity with risky options has been shown to result in reduced perceptions of their riskiness, a process by which familiarity may breed liking (Weber, Siebenmorgen, and Weber 2005). Once differences in risk perception between women and men are properly taken into account, the gender differences in risk attitude (defined as the trade-off between perceived risks and benefits) disappear.

To see why even small differences in risk perception between men and women may lead to significant differences in financial outcomes in real life, it is instructive to review Farrell's (2011, 2014) work. By combining the results of the Florida State Board of Administration's Investment Plan Data and the Florida Department of Education's Employee Survey in the third quarter of 2008, Farrell analyzed the pension plan investments of approximately 34,000 state employees. **Figure 2** shows the average expected portfolio standard deviation and the average allocation to risky assets of pension plan participants by gender and culture.

FIGURE 2. PORTFOLIO RISK CHARACTERISTICS BY GENDER AND CULTURE

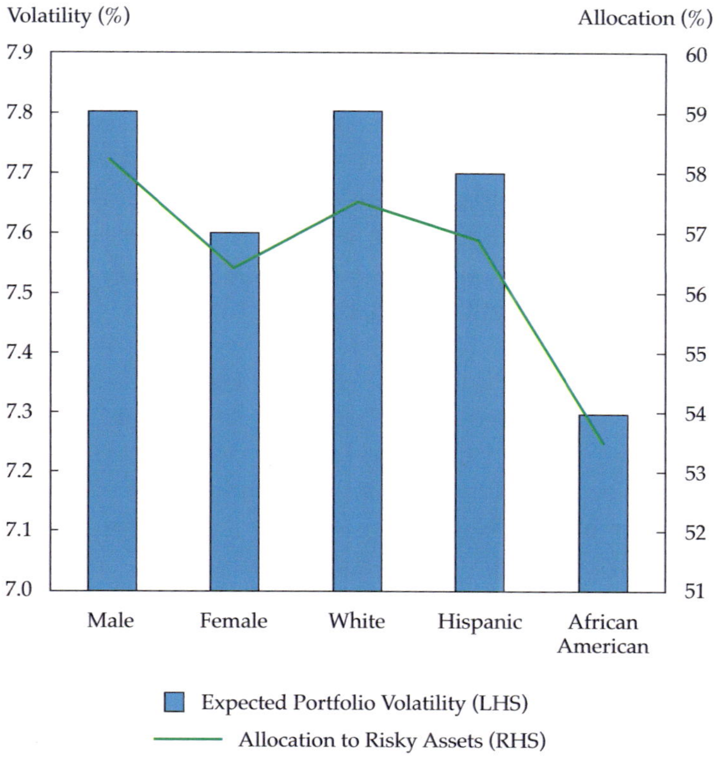

Source: Farrell (2014).

When saving for retirement, these small differences can have a big effect. Farrell (2014) estimates that if employees of the Florida Department of Education save 9% of their annual salary of approximately $34,000 for retirement, after 30 years of service the average white man would end up with a lump sum of $200,833 in real terms, whereas the average African-American woman would end up with $186,761 (93% of the white man's wealth at retirement). If these retirement lump sums are converted into an annuity plan that pays 50% of pre-retirement income, a white man would receive income for 17.6 years and an African-American woman would receive sufficient income for 15.6 years—despite the fact that women have longer life expectancies than men.

As Garnick (2016) points out, most women in the workplace are affected by a triple whammy. First, they have fewer years of service before retirement because they take time off to have children or care for parents and other relatives. Second, they earn less money than men, on average. Third, they are more risk averse with their retirement savings. These three factors combine to create a smaller retirement nest egg for women. Once retired, women are again at a disadvantage—a fourth whammy—because of their longer life expectancy and higher healthcare costs (women live longer but are not necessarily healthier in old age).

These findings can provide guidance for financial advisers on how to engage with both women and men. Men tend to be more optimistic about the prospects of financial investments than women. Educating men about the particular risks of an investment will likely reduce this over-optimism. In contrast, women tend to perceive greater risks in their investment decisions . Educating women about the risks (or the lack thereof) and correcting their assessment of how likely these risks are to materialize will overcome some of the gender differences in risk taking.

The empirical data make clear that one of the key responsibilities of financial advisers is to nudge women toward increased retirement savings (not only in tax-advantaged accounts) and increased risk in their long-term investments. Advisers certainly should not push women into reckless investments with unjustified risks; instead, they should educate female clients about the long-term effects of their investment choices and help them become more familiar—and hence comfortable—with a higher allocation to sound long-term investment portfolios and additional savings.

CULTURAL DIFFERENCES

Just as differences in risk perception between women and men contribute to gender differences in risk taking, differences in perceived risk and their effects on risk taking have also been systematically observed across cultures. Weber and Hsee (1998) investigated the risk attitudes in financial decisions of individuals in the United States, the People's Republic of China, Poland, and Germany. They found that Chinese investors were systematically more likely to engage in risky investments than US investors. The variation between different cultures was significantly more than the variations within a given culture, and Chinese investors were willing to pay higher prices for risky investments than investors in the United States or Germany. Again, these cultural differences were mainly driven by differences in risk perception. Because of their extensive social networks that cushion them against experiencing extreme losses in their investments, Chinese investors perceived a given investment option as less risky than US investors, leading to a higher propensity to invest and a willingness to pay a higher price for the investment.

More recently, Wang, Rieger, and Hens (2009) investigated time preferences in 45 countries. Investors were given a choice between a payment of \$100 now or a payment of *X* in 1 year from now or, in a separate question, in 10 years from now. The investors then had to provide the number *X* (presumably >\$100) that would make the two options equally attractive to them. The results allowed the researchers to identify time preferences and implicit discount rates for future cash flows. **Figure 3** shows that respondents from Germanic and Nordic countries (such as Germany, Switzerland, and Sweden) had systematically lower discount rates, which implies that investors from these countries were more likely to wait for a future cash flow than to opt for an immediate payout. Investors in Anglo-Saxon countries showed similar discount rates to Nordic and Germanic investors but were somewhat less likely to wait for a future payout given a specific alternative. The groups of investors that showed the highest-discount rates, who were thus least likely to invest for the long term, were located in Africa and Eastern Europe.

Again, as in the case of gender differences, the main driver behind the willingness to wait for a larger future cash flow instead of an immediate smaller cash flow was the

FIGURE 3. IMPLICIT DISCOUNT RATES IN DIFFERENT CULTURES

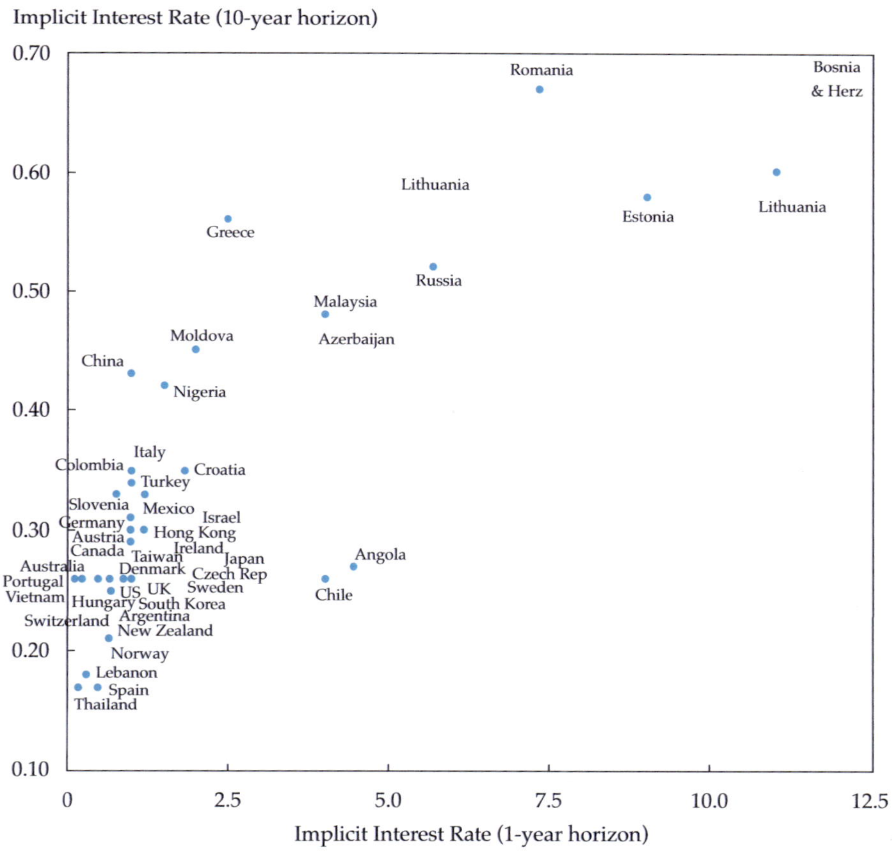

Source: Wang, Rieger, and Hens (2009).

perceived risk of the future cash flow. The researchers found that investors in cultures that—rightly or wrongly—perceived greater uncertainty around delayed cash flows were more likely to opt for immediate cash flows. Other cultural traits, such as individualism or long-term orientation, also played a role in determining the differences in perceptions of risk and uncertainty between cultures.

Notably, these cross-cultural differences may be driven not only by systematic cultural influences but also by current and recent economic circumstances. Such countries as Bosnia/Herzegovina, Russia, Angola, and Nigeria showed extremely high discount rates. Investors in these countries may be culturally different from investors in Germany or the United States. But such countries as Bosnia, Russia, and Nigeria are also characterized by high political and societal instability. It is only rational for an investor in a country where the government can confiscate private property at any time or where a civil war may erupt to prefer immediate cash flows. The stable legal, economic, and political framework observed in Scandinavia, Western Europe, and North America is certainly conducive to a lower level of risk perception. Similarly, more collectivist cultures or more tight-knit communities provide implicit insurance against financial risks (a social "cushion" by which community members help each other out in case of experienced losses), thus objectively reducing the risks and increasing risk taking (Weber and Hsee 1998) and decreasing the discounting of future rewards (Jachimowicz, Chafik, Munrat, Prabhu, and Weber 2017).

CONCLUSION: WHAT'S AN ADVISER TO DO?

The reviewed literature shows that risk attitudes, properly defined, are more or less stable throughout an investor's lifetime. These studies also show, however, that an important second determinant of risk aversion or risk taking is driven more by circumstances than by traits. Recent market events and investors' lifetime experiences do influence investment decisions because they change the perception of risk.[1] Financial advisers need to regularly assess these changing risk perceptions in order to provide the best possible advice for their clients. Without being too formulaic, we think that advisers can take four steps to help clients improve their investment decisions.

1. BE AWARE

Financial advisers need to be aware of their clients' base risk attitude and their potential systematic biases in their perception of risk. Risk attitude can be elicited through

[1]Malmendier and Nagel (2011) demonstrate the role lifetime experiences can play in changing risk perception.

simple survey questions and is relatively stable over time. Systematic biases in risk perception may result from gender, minority status within a society, lifetime experiences in financial markets, or recent market events. Differences in risk perception as the result of these variables can be elicited through appropriate survey questions that allow for the expression of subjective or emotional factors or simply by looking at the actual investment decisions investors have made in the past or their current investment portfolios, factoring in their known and stable attitudes toward risk.

2. EDUCATE

Educating clients about financial market risks is a vital ingredient for improving investment decisions. A key component of financial education is to demonstrate the differences between short-term and long-term outcomes of risky investments. A good understanding of the true riskiness of different investments for both short-term and long-term investments lays the groundwork for better decisions.

Advisers should not expect too much from education, however. Learning about investments is a higher cognitive process, and the research reviewed here has shown that short-term emotional reactions can easily override such "rational" considerations.

3. NUDGE

Nudging investors toward sensible investment decisions can go a long way to improve financial outcomes. These nudges can take many different forms. Pension plan sponsors are now well aware of the power of the default investment option for plan participants. By choosing a well-diversified portfolio of assets as the default option, many plan participants will end up with a portfolio that may be less than optimal but that will at least provide decent long-run outcomes.

But nudging investors toward better investment decisions can take much simpler forms. Most advisers present their clients with annual or quarterly investment statements. If quarterly investment results are shown in isolation, the investor's time horizon is immediately reduced to a three-month period. If, however, the quarterly results are put into a long-term financial context—for example, by showing the latest quarterly results in a chart with the expected long-term development of the portfolio over the next 10 or 20 years—then short-term fluctuations in the portfolio appear much less daunting and much less relevant for the long-term success of a chosen portfolio. Optics matter, and with the right presentation style, financial advisers can help their clients focus on long-term investment outcomes rather than short-term market fluctuations.

4. HOLD HANDS

Abraham Lincoln referred to an ancient Persian adage during a speech in 1859:

> It is said an Eastern monarch once charged his wise men to invent him a sentence, to be ever in view, and which should be true and appropriate in all times and situations. They presented him the words: "And this, too, shall pass away." How much it expresses! How chastening in the hour of pride! How consoling in the depths of affliction! (Lincoln 1859)

Conveying this motto to clients should be part of the daily work of every financial adviser.

Managing investor emotions through the ups and downs of financial markets is arguably a financial adviser's most important task. The groundwork needs to be laid in calm times when investments are doing well, when advisers need to prepare their clients for the inevitable turbulence that will come in the future and the emotional responses that go along with it. These calm times provide an opportunity to discuss and formulate an investment policy for each client that can be consulted when emotions are running high.

When times are good, a financial adviser's first task is to keep expectations under control. Clients may become greedy or simply too optimistic about the future when risks are perceived to be low or minimal. Similarly, in a market downturn or in a market crisis, a financial adviser's first task is to boost optimism. Risk perceptions in these situations are high, and most investment options appear too risky. In these times, the focus should be on the long-term opportunities of different investments as well as the increased return potential. If the groundwork has been laid properly—by formulating a long-term investment policy, by educating clients about the riskiness of investments in the short term and the long term, and by limiting over-optimism when times are good—it is much easier for an adviser to convince clients that things will eventually get better.

Too often, financial advisers define their main responsibility as finding the right investment products and building the best portfolio for their clients. As we have illustrated, the best investment portfolio might not help a client whose risk perceptions change dramatically in different financial market circumstances. When emotions run high, even the best portfolio might be abandoned, leaving the client with inferior investment outcomes. Managing risk perceptions requires the financial adviser to act more like a therapist than a mechanic. It is above all about managing expectations and emotions and helping clients to better deal with emotions when it comes to financial decisions. The end result of this process might be a portfolio that is not "optimal" in the sense of modern portfolio theory, with its assumption of econs, but rather a portfolio that "satisfies" the human need for investments that can be handled in the presence of changing emotions and changing risk perceptions.

REFERENCES

Benartzi, S., and R.H. Thaler. 1995. "Myopic Loss Aversion and the Equity Premium Puzzle." *Quarterly Journal of Economics* 110 (1): 73–92.

Byrnes, J.P., D.C. Miller, and W.D. Schafer. 1999. "Gender Differences in Risk Taking: A Meta-Analysis." *Psychological Bulletin* 125 (3): 367–83.

Davies, G.B. 2017. *New Vistas in Risk Profiling*. Charlottesville, VA: CFA Institute Research Foundation.

ESMA. 2017. "Consultation Paper on Guidelines on Certain Aspects of the MiFID II Suitability Requirements." ESMA 35-43-748.

European Parliament and European Council. 2004. Markets in Financial Instruments Directive. Directive 2004/39/EC.

European Parliament and European Council. 2006. Markets in Financial Instruments Directive: Implementing Directive. Commission Directive 2006/73/EC.

Farrell, J. 2011. "Demographics of Risky Investing." *Research in Business and Economics Journal*, Special Edition, Florida Economic Symposium.

Farrell, J. 2014. "Demographic and Socioeconomic Factors of Investors." In *Investor Behavior*, edited by H.K. Baker and V. Ricciardi, 117–134. Hoboken, NJ: John Wiley & Sons.

Feldman Barrett, L. 2017. *How Emotions Are Made*. New York: Houghton Mifflin Harcourt.

Garnick, D. 2016. *Income Insights: Gender Retirement Gap*. TIAA.

Grable, J.E. 2016. "Financial Risk Tolerance." In *Handbook of Consumer Finance Research*, edited by J.J. Xiao, 19–31. Cham, Switzerland: Springer International Publishing.

Grable, J.E. 2017. *Financial Risk Tolerance: A Psychometric Review*. Charlottesville, VA: CFA Institute Research Foundation.

Hirshleifer, D., and T. Shumway. 2003. "Good Day Sunshine: Stock Returns and the Weather." *Journal of Finance* 58 (3): 1009–32.

Hoffmann, A.O.I., T. Post, and J.M.E. Pennings. 2015. "How Investor Perceptions Drive Actual Trading and Risk-Taking Behavior." *Journal of Behavioral Finance* 16 (1): 94–103.

Jachimowicz, J.M., S. Chafik, S. Munrat, J. Prabhu, and E.U. Weber. 2017. "Community Trust Reduces Myopic Decisions in Low-Income Individuals." *Proceedings of the National Academy of Sciences of the United States of America* 114: 5401–06.

Lincoln, A. 1859. *Address before the Wisconsin State Agricultural Society.* www.abrahamlincolnonline.org/lincoln/speeches/fair.htm.

Loewenstein, G.F., E.U. Weber, C.K. Hsee, and N. Welch. 2001. "Risks as Feelings." *Psychological Bulletin* 127: 267–86.

Malmendier, U., and S. Nagel. 2011. "Depression Babies: Do Macroeconomic Experiences Affect Risk-Taking?" *Quarterly Journal of Economics* 126 (1): 373–416.

Markowitz, H. 1952. "Portfolio Selection." *Journal of Finance* 7: 77–91.

Nguyen, L.T.M., G. Gallery, and C. Newton. 2017. "The Influence of Financial Risk Tolerance on Investment Decision-Making in a Financial Advice Context." *Australasian Accounting, Business and Finance Journal* 10 (3): 3–22.

Sahm, C.R. 2008. "How Much Does Risk Tolerance Change?" Working paper, Finance and Economics Discussion Series, Division of Research & Statistics and Monetary Affairs, Federal Reserve Board.

Thaler, R.H. 2015. *Misbehaving: The Making of Behavioral Economics.* London: Allen Lane.

Wang, M., M.O. Rieger, and T. Hens. 2009. *How Time Preferences Differ: Evidence from 45 Countries.* Swiss Finance Institute, Research Paper No. 09-47.

Weber, E.U., A.-R. Blais, and N. Betz. 2002. "A Domain-Specific Risk-Attitude Scale: Measuring Risk Perceptions and Risk Behaviors." *Journal of Behavioral Decision Making* 15: 263–90.

Weber, E.U., and C.K. Hsee. 1998. "Cross-Cultural Differences in Risk Perception but Cross-Cultural Similarities in Attitudes towards Risk." *Management Science* 44 (9): 1205–17.

Weber, E.U., and E.J. Johnson. 2008. "Decisions under Uncertainty: Psychological, Economic, and Neuroeconomic Explanations of Risk Preference." In *Neuroeconomics: Decision Making and the Brain,* edited by P. Glimcher, C. Camerer, E. Fehr, and R. Poldrack, 127–144. New York: Elsevier.

Weber, E.U., and R.A. Milliman. 1997. "Perceived Risk Attitudes: Relating Risk Perception to Risky Choice." *Management Science* 43 (2): 123–44.

Weber, E.U., N. Siebenmorgen, and M. Weber. 2005. "Communicating Asset Risk: How Name Recognition and the Format of Historic Volatility Information Affect Risk Perception and Investment Decisions." *Risk Analysis* 25 (3): 597–609.

Weber, M., E.U. Weber, and A. Nosić. 2013. "Who Takes Risks When and Why: Determinants of Changes in Investor Risk Taking." *Review of Finance* 17 (3): 847–83.

NEW VISTAS IN RISK PROFILING

Greg B. Davies

A CONFUSED LANDSCAPE

Risk profiling is one of the most fundamental aspects of determining a suitable investment solution for an individual. It is also one of the most misunderstood.

This situation results in many ill-advised approaches, both to determining various components of a client's risk profile and to using them in arriving at an appropriate solution.

Among these ill-advised approaches are

- using a client's actual behaviour (their "revealed preferences") to determine the *risk tolerance* used to construct their long-term portfolio;
- using components of a client's attitudes toward risk other than long-term risk tolerance as inputs into portfolio "optimisation," rather than helping the client to mitigate and control them;
- trying to elicit risk tolerance on subcomponents of a client's overall wealth, rather than as a feature of the person as a whole;
- using over-engineered and unstable approaches to establishing risk tolerance when simpler measures would be not only sufficient but also better;
- putting too much effort into spuriously precise measures of risk tolerance and far too little into understanding *risk capacity*, which in many cases is the more important component of a *risk profile*; and
- using "required" returns as inputs to determine the investment solution, rather than guiding the client to reasonable expectations as an *outcome* of the client's circumstances and of the returns available in markets.

Much of the problem lies in the rather imprecise and ambiguous way the industry uses the terminology around risk profiling, with terms such as *risk tolerance*, *risk capacity*, *risk appetite*, and *risk attitude* applied to a range of different concepts in different parts of the world, in different organisations, and, indeed, sometimes within an organisation in different conversations with a single client.

However, even where terminology is stable, there are areas of confusion. For example, the industry lacks a coherent model of risk capacity and how it relates to risk tolerance (both as defined below). What gets measured gets managed, so risk tolerance is frequently called on to do much more work than it should in determining a suitable portfolio solution. Though a full model of risk capacity is beyond the scope of this article, it does have implications for how we think about risk tolerance and how we go about measuring it.

Also, there is a frequent tendency to use short-term behavioural responses in "optimising" a portfolio—that is, building a portfolio solution around the assumption that an investor's observed behaviour is somehow "desirable" and should be used as an input to the optimization process. Instead, one should try to make clients more comfortable with a long-term approach that treats such responses as undesirable. For example, attempts to use *loss aversion* or *ambiguity aversion* as inputs into an optimal portfolio solution often fail to recognize that there are aspects of risk attitudes that are helpful in determining the "right" investment and that there are aspects that are harmful. We should help investors to *overcome* the harmful ones to prevent their behavioural responses from getting in the way of good long-term outcomes. These aspects of the client's overall risk profile should refine, not define, the investment solution.[1]

In the first part of this article, I shall discuss how we should think about the crucial elements of (a) risk tolerance, (b) behavioural risk attitudes, and (c) risk capacity. In the second, I use a simple thought experiment to examine a stripped-down investor situation and define the essential features and exact role of each of the components of an investor's overall risk profile. In doing so, I shall use terminology that is broadly consistent with that used by regulators to stipulate how each concept should be used in delivering a *suitable* investment solution. For example, risk tolerance will refer to that subcomponent of risk attitudes that should be used in determining the long-term "right" investment solution, rather than to any attitude toward risk that the investor happens to have over the investment journey. Others may choose to apply different terms to concepts unearthed in the thought experiment; sadly, I suspect a globally consistent terminology might be too much to hope for. But if we can at least reach agreement on what the essential components are, however named, then we will have made progress.

Armed with a clear distinction of what we mean by the various elements of risk profiling, it becomes a much simpler task to ask how we might best go about eliciting these

[1]"Beyond Risk Profiling" (2015).

elements. The final part of the article will examine options for eliciting and measuring risk tolerance and will consider some promising avenues for future methods.

REVIEWING THE LANDSCAPE

To undertake risk profiling effectively, we need to have a clear idea of what it is we're trying to understand. Broadly speaking, a comprehensive risk profile requires understanding two characteristics of a client:

1. their willingness to take risk
2. their ability to take risk[2]

But what exactly do we mean by these terms, and what do we need to understand about the client in order to put them to practical use?

WILLINGNESS TO TAKE RISK

The first aspect, willingness to take risk, is often variously, and ambiguously, referred to as risk attitude, risk tolerance, risk aversion, or risk appetite. In a sense, it doesn't matter too much what we call it. What is important is that there is a crucial distinction to be made between

a. *risk tolerance* (an investor's stable, reasoned willingness to take risk in the long term) and

b. *behavioural risk attitudes* (the unstable, behavioural, short-term willingness to take risk exhibited through an investor's actions—i.e., the investor's "revealed" preferences).

From the perspective of investment suitability, the former reflects the normative level of risk we should seek to deliver for a client over the long term.

[2]Required or desired returns typically should *not* form part of an investor's risk profile. In the vast majority of cases, these should be determined by whatever expected returns might be attained through efficient use of the client's appropriate risk level, which is in turn determined by his risk capacity and risk tolerance. For most of the population, the appropriate level is the highest amount of risk that can be taken given both willingness and capacity to take risk; one of the two will be a biting constraint. If a client's goals are too expensive for either her willingness or capacity to take risk, then the goals should be adjusted, not the risk profile. Increasing risk to attain "required" returns inappropriately increases the chances of catastrophic failure to reach all goals. Only where both capacity and willingness are high relative to the future needs and goals of the investor (usually only the case for particularly wealthy individuals) will there be sufficient slack in the system for required returns to be useful. Even then, there is an argument for still basing the risk level on risk tolerance, since this will provide the best security against future changes in the investor's goals and preferences.

The latter, in contrast, frequently reflects transient and context-dependent preferences[3] that would result in poor satisfaction of the investor's long-term needs if we mistakenly take them to be a guide to long-term risk preferences.[4]

This second set may contain a whole range of different influences on risk attitude, including loss aversion, ambiguity aversion, risk perceptions, and probability distortion. Apart from being unstable, these are also context dependent, myopic, present biased, and procyclical and often lead to absurd levels of risk aversion when aggregated. They are not attitudes we should want in the driver's seat for our long-term portfolio optimisation. If used to determine the "suitable" risk level of the portfolio, these attitudes can deliver an undesirable long-term solution based on an assessment of fleeting point-in-time preferences, with on average a much lower level of risk than the investor's own long-term willingness to take risk and with the added danger of buying low and selling high.

In the end, the role of suitability is to steer investors to better outcomes, not replicate (and optimise for) all the silly things they do already.

ABILITY TO TAKE RISK

In addition to ascertaining how much risk investors are willing to take, it is important to understand how much risk they are *able* to take. This concept also goes by many loosely defined labels, such as risk capacity, capacity for loss, and ability to bear loss. At their core, these are all variations on the underlying notion that the amount of risk an investor might be willing to take could nonetheless be ill-advised if it endangers the investor's ability to fund future financial commitments from the portfolio. I shall refer to this notion as *risk capacity* throughout this article, using it to encompass all the terms listed above.

Since risk capacity concerns the investor's ability to meet any future liabilities,[5] it depends on a number of elements of the investor's holistic financial position. These all help determine the degree to which the investor will be able to continue to fund future required cash flows in the event his portfolio value declines:

- First, the size of the total investable assets relative to total net wealth. Investable assets are where the investment risk resides, so the fewer investable assets clients have relative to other assets, the higher their capacity to take risk. Investors who invest only a small portion of their net wealth have more capacity to take risk

[3]Payne, Bettman, and Schkade (1999); Slovic (1995).

[4]Odean (1999); Davies and de Servigny (2012), chaps. 2 and 5.

[5]Apart from some infrequent circumstances where a future commitment can only be funded from a specific pool of assets.

without jeopardising future commitments. The value of these other assets may vary substantially in value and indeed is only likely to be realised when the investor's circumstances are pressured. This implies that a very conservative assessment of the value of non-investment wealth is appropriate. Nonetheless, an investor with other wealth to fall back on will have greater risk capacity than one who doesn't.

- Second, the degree to which the investor is willing or able to realise the value in non-investment assets to cover liabilities in the event that they can't be funded from the investment portfolio. More liquid assets, and those practically and emotionally easier to sell if circumstances require doing so, will provide more risk capacity than those the investor can't or won't realise the value of until they are in dire straits.

- Third, the degree to which future spending might be met using the client's expected future income,[6] which may be thought of as *human capital* or *net future wealth*. It depends on the following:

    - Future income expectations: More certain and stable future income will more reliably increase risk capacity than variable or uncertain income streams (e.g., don't count too much on distant inheritance expectations when determining today's risk capacity).

    - The future liabilities themselves: The greater an investor's goals and spending needs, the more her investment portfolio needs to provide for and, therefore, the lower her capacity to place the capital value at risk. Note that in this sense, the greater the wealth "required" to fund future liabilities, the *lower* the capacity to take risk, contrary to many approaches that use "required returns" as an excuse to *increase* portfolio risk.

    - Flexibility regarding future liabilities and expenses: If the investor has discretion over whether to incur a future expense, then expenses can be reduced or delayed in the event of poor market performance. Such an investor thus has greater risk capacity.

These last elements show the essential, and close, connection between any reasonable assessment of risk capacity and both (a) a truly holistic view of the client's current circumstances and (b) a coherent approach to goal-based investing. Risk capacity, correctly conceived, is the vital pivot between goal-based cash-flow-planning approaches and investment solutions. It turns the information gleaned from a thorough planning process into a measure that helps define the appropriate level of risk for the investment process.

[6]And the degree to which unexpected future liabilities are insured against.

Interestingly, this observation also reveals that even risk capacity, usually thought of as being about the investor's objective financial circumstances, is strongly behavioural. One of the most effective routes to increasing risk capacity is to manage client aspirations, expectations, goals, and future financial commitments. The less you want, the more you can take risk to grow your wealth and the more you may wind up with.

As mentioned, this article is not the place to develop a full framework for measuring risk capacity. However, understanding what it is—and isn't—is vital to being able to approach a client's willingness to take risk and to understand some of the future directions for assessing risk tolerance. It also helps us understand why developing ever more precise measures of risk tolerance may not be the best use of resources.

For most investors, risk capacity is overwhelmingly more important than risk tolerance; the right level of risk for their investments is far more likely to be constrained by their lack of capacity to cope with capital losses than by their psychological aversion to long-term risk.[7] And yet, because it is inherently more difficult to measure, with more moving parts, risk capacity is also largely neglected.

The relative importance of getting risk capacity and risk tolerance right is related to the ratio of the *flow* of income and expenditure to the *stock* of wealth. Investors with small flows in and out of their balance sheet relative to the size of the balance sheet (typically very wealthy people with large net asset values) will be likely to have high risk capacity, since they have significant wealth with which to fund future liabilities as they arise. For them, risk tolerance is far more likely to be the binding constraint.

For most investors, however, the future expenditures they will have to fund from their investible assets are substantial relative to their stock of wealth. For them, risk capacity is a far more important notion than risk tolerance, and yet it is one that many investment suitability processes largely gloss over. Even investors with high willingness to take risk should avoid doing so if the potential losses will mean they're unlikely to be able to fund future commitments. And yet the bulk of the industry debate (to which, admittedly, this article is contributing) is devoted to how to better measure risk tolerance, a stable feature of someone's personality easily measured to an adequate degree of accuracy with a simple psychometric scale.

However, part of the reason there is little agreement on how to categorise risk capacity and the two broad categories of risk attitudes (risk tolerance and behavioural responses) is that all of this appears hugely complicated. It is very easy for confusion to arise or for those with vested interests in particular views to obfuscate the debate. So, let us try to

[7]Short-term risk preferences are another matter, but they often lead to the investor not taking enough risk and making mistakes along the journey, rather than being a reason not to take risk.

isolate each of these three components with a thought experiment that strips away all the extraneous detail and allows us to focus on the essential features.

A RISK-PROFILING THOUGHT EXPERIMENT

Let us first imagine the simplest possible hypothetical investment situation for a single investor, Christy, and ask what the notions of risk tolerance and risk capacity mean in this context. Then we will gradually add features to the example to see what insights we can glean.

CASE 1: ISOLATING RISK TOLERANCE

Let's assume that Christy has a single portfolio of investable assets (for the simplicity of a round number, let's assume $1 million) that she wishes to invest for a fixed period of 10 years.

She has no need to draw income from the portfolio: All her future spending needs are exactly covered by her future income, and she is fully insured against any unexpected financial needs. She also has no other assets or liabilities. After 10 years she will collect the investment and move on to invest elsewhere. She will have no need at that point to withdraw or spend any part of the portfolio.

These assumptions remove, for now, considerations of risk capacity. Christy is investing the totality of her wealth, current and future, and there are no possible future financial commitments that would be jeopardised by losses, either through the 10-year period or at the end.

While this is a highly stylized and unrealistic scenario, it helps strip a complex problem back to its essentials to understand what really matters. Also, this is not much more than advisers often know about a client who brings them a portfolio to invest and doesn't wish to disclose much information about their broader financial situation or future goals. The bulk of the work in determining what is suitable has to be done by a risk-profiling process.

In addition, imagine at this point, for the sake of simplicity, that Christy will act completely on your recommendation for how the money should be invested and will pay no attention whatsoever to the portfolio in the intervening 10 years. These last assumptions are crucial for eliminating the possibility of behavioural responses to initiating the investment or to the investment journey.

What is the right level of risk for Christy's portfolio?

This bare-bones investment scenario is designed to isolate the role of risk tolerance. Risk capacity is neutralised, and emotional or behavioural aspects of risk attitude are neutralised. All that matters is Christy's willingness (now) to trade off the future chance of good financial outcomes for the possibility of bad outcomes. This is the type of problem envisioned in Markowitz's mean–variance analysis—finding an optimal trade-off between risk and return to suit the long-term risk tolerance of the investor.

Because only long-term outcomes matter, any measure of risk tolerance that is unstable, dependent on Christy's current context or emotional state, or influenced by the current state of the market is going to result in a portfolio aiming for the wrong target. And in this scenario, Christy won't even notice valuations along the way, so trying to incorporate any behavioural features that depend on her current reference point (e.g., loss aversion) will be inappropriate. What *is* required in this pure example is an assessment now of her deeply held and, as far as possible, stable preferences for trading off risk and return of long-term future outcomes. In other words, we need to assess her risk tolerance as an underlying psychological trait. In this example, nothing else matters. Fortunately there is a great deal of evidence that when examined using psychometric approaches, risk tolerance is both a measurable and stable trait.[8]

We cannot elicit the risk tolerance trait we need by observing investment choices, either real or through hypothetical questions put to investors; there are problems in extrapolating both long-term preferences from short-term choices[9] and aggregate preferences from choices over subcomponents.[10] Current choices may tell us quite accurately what risks people *do* take but not what risk trade-off we should optimise for when building their long-term portfolio. The latter is what is required from a risk tolerance measure.

CASE 2: INTRODUCING RISK CAPACITY

Now let's add one complication to the scenario and see how it differs from the situation above. Imagine that at the end of the 10 years, Christy will be *required* to purchase a single asset with the full amount of the portfolio as it stands at that date. This scenario, for example, was to some degree the case until recently in UK pensions, where many investors were compelled to purchase an annuity with their pension pot at retirement.[11] Does this change the risk that it is appropriate to take with her investments?

---

[8]For example, see Weber, Weber, and Nosić (2013); Davies and Brooks (2014); Sahm (2012); Egan, Davies, and Brooks (2011).

[9]For example, Benartzi and Thaler (1995); Samuelson (1963).

[10]For example, Thaler (1999); Rabin (2000).

[11]In reality the rules were more complex. For example, 25% of the value could be taken tax free as cash, and full compulsion for annuitisation was for those over 75.

The answer is yes, very significantly. This simple change sets up a future liability to be funded from the portfolio. It has no effect on Christy's risk tolerance, but it reduces her risk capacity. More importantly, it reduces her risk capacity in a dynamic way. Initially the effect on the appropriate risk level would be small. Ten years is a long way off, and initially almost all that would matter is her risk tolerance, as before. Christy would want to maximise her risk–return trade-off to get the best possible future outcome relative to her risk tolerance. As the date approaches, however, it would become increasingly important not to expose the capital value to the whims of the market. In particular, in the days leading up to the termination date, she would wish to reduce the risk level to zero to ensure she wasn't forced to sell at a low value just because the markets happened to have dropped that week or even that day.[12]

This, broadly, is the rational justification for target-date funds (TDFs), which—as originally conceived—gradually reduce risk to zero by a specific date (usually related to retirement).[13] However, there are two big problems with such funds. The lesser problem is that they tend to reduce risk linearly with time even though risk capacity doesn't reduce linearly but, rather, accelerates to zero as the final date approaches. The more important problem is that target-date funds are an ideal solution only for an ideal case: The moment the investor's situation becomes more complex than that of needing to fund a single asset purchase at a single termination date, such funds will deliver the wrong answer. The usual result is that most investors take substantially less risk than they should.

Note that in this scenario *nothing* about Christy's risk tolerance changes, and yet the appropriate solution changes dramatically. Indeed, over much of the life of the portfolio, the suitable answer will be driven much more by an assessment of risk capacity than by risk tolerance. Also, the risk capacity will change in a fairly systematic and measurable (indeed, to a large extent predictable) way with time, which means that the solution can be dynamically adjusted without any need for subsequent profiling.

The difference between these two situations can also be interpreted in terms of *time horizon* (another widely misunderstood notion in suitability). In the first case, Christy's true investment horizon is indefinite, despite leaving her assets with the investment manager for only 10 years; her investing is a going concern throughout, and beyond, the engagement.[14] In the second case, her investment horizon is 10 years initially and decreases steadily as that date approaches.

---

[12]Indeed, some of the biggest losers from the financial crisis were those exposed to risk assets in late 2008 and early 2009 and who were forced to annuitize this value during this time.

[13]In current practice, many TDFs never reach zero risk because the managers believe that even retirees need to take some risk—for example, to keep up with inflation.

[14]This point, however, raises a complication. The investment manager will want to deliver a good outcome at the point Christy will remove assets and thus will be incentivised to reduce risk as the 10-year point approaches, despite the fact that doing so is not at all in Christy's best interest.

CASE 3: MULTIPLE FIXED GOALS

Now let's add a further complication: Assume that every year along the way Christy will need to withdraw $50,000 from her portfolio. This sets up a chain of nine additional liabilities, which has a (negative) effect on her risk capacity. But, interestingly, it may also have implications for how we assess risk tolerance.

These liabilities may be seen as additional goals that Christy needs to achieve along the journey. Each is relatively small compared to the initial portfolio value of $1 million, but the higher the level of portfolio risk, the greater the chance that any given withdrawal will take a large chunk out of the portfolio if valuations are low at that point—making a good final value much harder to achieve.

As with the final asset purchase (a withdrawal of 100% of remaining portfolio value at the termination), each of these withdrawals will play a successively larger role in reducing risk capacity as they get closer to occurring. Each future liability will reduce risk capacity according to (a) how large it is and (b) how close it is in time.[15] If Christy has no anticipation of withdrawing from the portfolio to spend (as in Case 1), then her risk capacity is extremely high; if she needs to withdraw it all to spend tomorrow (as she would at the end of the 10 years in Case 2), then her risk capacity is near zero; for all intermediate cases, her risk capacity is reduced insofar as spending needs are larger and closer.[16]

Armed with this notion, it also becomes reasonably clear how we would adapt Case 1 to deal with any withdrawals Christy may plan to make *after* the end of the 10-year period. Such withdrawals will reduce her risk capacity, but because they are a long way off, their initial effect will be muted.

A big drop in portfolio value will mean that each subsequent $50,000 withdrawal becomes a larger percentage of the total portfolio, with the effect that these withdrawals will further reduce risk capacity.[17] In this scenario, the risk profile of the portfolio can still be adjusted automatically to provide the appropriate solution, without any recourse to further client profiling, as long as we can fully describe her financial circumstances and withdrawal needs. Everything we need to know about Christy in this scenario is defined by her circumstances (for risk capacity) and her risk tolerance.

[15]And, as we shall see in Case 4, also by how malleable this cash is with regard to timing, magnitude, or necessity.

[16]This concept would need to be expanded upon if we extended the example to allow Christy to have other assets and liabilities on her balance sheet and additional income and expenditure cash flows over time.

[17]An interesting corollary that follows from this notion is that a coherent model of risk capacity is very closely related to the ongoing debates around *sequencing risk* and should provide a useful tool in deriving appropriate solutions to this problem.

CASE 4: CONTINGENT GOALS

Now let's let Christy back in along the journey—but not fully. Let's still imagine she's immune to any emotional responses to her portfolio value over the journey—no doubt, no anxiety, no loss aversion, no panic—but she may decide to change her withdrawal amounts along the journey in response to how her portfolio is doing. If it is doing well, she may decide to increase the withdrawal beyond her planned $50,000; if it is doing badly, she may decrease the withdrawal or potentially forgo it altogether.

As well as providing a means to respond dynamically to changing circumstances, this example also enables Christy to place different levels of *priority* on these interim goals/withdrawals. When she has no ability to modify or forgo interim withdrawals, we have in effect assumed that Christy sees each of these withdrawals as equally vital, which, because they occur earlier, implies that she gives them priority over achieving a good final value of the portfolio. When we allow her to modify or forgo these interim goals, we are instead implicitly saying that she may see these as less important than maintaining the final value of the portfolio.

This flexibility means she is able to treat her goals (or at least some of them) as *contingent*—similar to a charity tasked with trying to maintain the capital value of its endowment over time by varying its spending according to the realised portfolio value. This is a highly sensible way of varying the sequencing of withdrawals since, on balance, it means selling more when values are high and retaining more capital in the fund when values are low. This plan may be constrained by certain baseline spending requirements, but it is seldom the case that we have no ability to tighten our belts a little when circumstances require it.

As an alternative way of seeing this, imagine that Christy has vague plans to use a large amount of her portfolio—say, $500,000—to put toward a second home in 12 years' time. Should this goal feature strongly in reducing her risk capacity? Probably not. Because her goal is still quite fuzzy, she has plenty of opportunity to change it in response to future circumstances. If her financial position is less strong than she had hoped as the time approaches, she could choose not to buy a house, she could purchase a smaller, cheaper house, or she could put the plans on ice and delay the purchase until her portfolio recovers.

The ability to vary our spending according to circumstances provides psychological and financial *optionality*. The option value of this flexibility is extremely large. It increases risk capacity because we no longer have to assume that we must blindly meet every spending goal regardless of circumstances. In practical terms, we shouldn't count the full value of future liabilities that are low priority, flexible, or contingent; this ability to adapt increases risk capacity. Many future goals will be contingent and low priority, and Christy should not dramatically shy away from taking risk now to protect capital for future plans that might not happen.

The ability to shrink or postpone goals if things don't turn out as we want means that we can afford to offer any future goal slightly less than full, unconditional protection. We thus make our finances more adaptable to changing circumstances, as well as to our own changing preferences and priorities. As things change, we can redeploy capital to those goals that are more important to us and shrink, delay, or forgo spending on goals that are no longer high priorities.

This is a major reason why we cannot truly assess risk capacity without embracing goal-based investing. It is also a major reason why most conventional approaches to goal-based investing,[18] which encourage investors to divide assets into "pots" to achieve individual spending goals, are sorely misguided. They encourage investors to be overly precise in their goals, and they reduce both the financial and psychological flexibility of being able to treat goals contingently and to transfer capital flexibly between goals as circumstances arise.[19]

Goals as a Component of Risk Profiling

But what about risk tolerance? This is the idea that the degree to which Christy's future goals affect her risk capacity depends on the importance she places on them and the degree to which she is prepared to postpone or shrink them, and it is a vital missing link in establishing her appropriate overall risk profile. It implies that we will never have a comprehensive description of the right investment risk level by just using a combination of risk tolerance and static risk capacity. Indeed, it is in the description of someone's overall *system* of goals, with all the valuable fuzziness and imprecision that this requires, that the notions of risk capacity and risk tolerance start to overlap and blur.

On the one hand, we have the concept of risk tolerance, which, as in Case 1, tells us how Christy views the trade-off of risk versus return for her indefinite-horizon investing—that is, investing that doesn't serve any specific withdrawal need and thus has no particular time horizon. On the other hand, we have the concept of risk capacity, which tells us how to decrease this risk level to protect future spending requirements depending on her weighted time horizon of future withdrawals[20] and how to change this risk depending on what else is on her balance sheet.

---

[18]Or attempts to apply liability-driven investment approaches to individual investors.

[19]See Brooks, Davies, and Smith (2015) for a behavioural perspective on goal-based investing.

[20]Or increase it if her future expected income flows outweigh her spending needs.

But between these we have the need to help Christy understand and articulate her system of goals, without imposing pressure for more precision than she feels is comfortable. This system of goals may be seen as a vital tool for establishing her risk capacity, accounting for the degree to which achieving each of her goals is essential to her. Without it, risk capacity won't provide an accurate description of the risk she can take.

But we can also see the description of her goals as a way of expressing more accurately her *tolerance* for risk: She should not be prepared to tolerate risks that place her coveted aspirations in danger or that place her cherished assets, her already achieved *crystallised goals*, at risk. Her risk tolerance could be reasonably viewed as an expression of the degree to which she is prepared to place a higher-priority goal at risk in order to have the chance of achieving both this more important goal and some other, less important goal as well. These may not be goals she can yet articulate or express, but ultimately, taking investment risk is a way to expand the set of financial goals one can attain while exposing oneself to the risk of shrinking this set. So risk tolerance, too, is about goals in the end.

The logical conclusion from this line of reasoning is that if we genuinely want to understand the right amount of risk for an investor to take, it is not sufficient just to measure risk tolerance. It is also not sufficient to supplement this with a narrow model of risk capacity. We fundamentally also need to help people understand, articulate, and dynamically adapt the totality of their future goals, plans, and aspirations over their journey.

Effective goal-based investing is the truly new vista in risk profiling.

CASE 5: BEHAVIOURAL ASPECTS OF RISK ATTITUDE

The last step we will take is to make Christy fully human. She now notices (sometimes) what is happening to her portfolio value, she concerns herself (sporadically) with the details of what her portfolio is invested in, and she has (frequent) behavioural and emotional responses to what happens over the investment journey. All of these cause her experienced risk attitudes to fluctuate at various points in time. Sometimes she acts on these fluctuations.

These *behavioural risk attitudes* may be considerably at odds with her underlying *risk tolerance* but nonetheless reflect how she feels about the risks she is taking at any given point in time. Christy, like all of us, is subject to anxiety, doubt, exuberance, myopia, and framing effects. It is impossible to deny that all these behavioural responses are a large part of her risk attitudes. It is also impossible to deny that these influence her decisions.

Understanding these ephemeral risk attitudes is thus an important part of any comprehensive risk-profiling exercise and should be used to guide investment advice. However, these behavioural aspects, revealed through observed behaviour, should not be used as the foundation for an assessment of risk tolerance and portfolio optimisation. Why would you "optimise" a risk–return trade-off for someone on the basis of all the error-prone, bias-ridden, context-dependent, pro-cyclical, unstable, myopic, and inconsistent behaviour they exhibit? Doing so is committing the *naturalistic fallacy*: You can't derive "ought" from "is." For example, we cannot infer from the fact that investors *do* exhibit loss aversion that these attitudes are what they *ought* to use to optimise their portfolio.

Risk tolerance is about Christy's willingness to accept risky *outcomes*, whereas these other behavioural aspects are more about her shorter-term emotional resilience along the journey. This distinction has huge ramifications for determining the correct investment solution and the degree to which risk attitudes should be built into portfolio solutions on the one hand or into the client relationship on the other. Risk tolerance, combined with her risk capacity, tells us what level of risk Christy *should* strive for in her portfolio. Her other behavioural risk attitudes instead affect her emotional comfort with this solution over the journey.

This doesn't mean we should ignore these risk attitudes, but we shouldn't pander to them either. Managing anxiety and emotional comfort along the journey are at least as important in attaining a good outcome as determining the "optimal" long-term solution. For example, using better client communication and long-term framing of investment performance reports may mitigate the emotional effects of loss aversion much more effectively and cheaply than changing the investment strategy to avoid instances of loss along the journey. No one will be completely comfortable with the compromises that have to be made in any investment program, so we should instead seek to make Christy *sufficiently* comfortable with a *sufficiently* efficient solution.[21]

We may draw a useful analogy between Christy's behavioural risk attitudes and her risk capacity. Just as risk capacity is affected by future financial liabilities that reduce her weighted time horizon of withdrawals, so her behavioural tendencies create the potential for future emotional liabilities (withdrawals) that reduce her emotional time horizon. Our human tendency to myopia and behavioural responses to our immediate environment means that in most cases we end up making decisions based on an emotional time horizon that is way shorter than our financial time horizon.

[21]See Davies (2014) for an extended discussion on how these behavioural tendencies can be measured using psychometric approaches and how these can be used to practically improve investors' emotional comfort.

As Keynes is reputed to have said (although there is no evidence that he actually did), "Markets can remain irrational for longer than you can remain solvent."[22] This is essentially an injunction to consider risk capacity when investing. The need to withdraw assets from your portfolio to meet a future liability (i.e., the need for financial liquidity) increases the risk of market values being "irrationally" low when this time comes; that is, it reduces risk capacity. However, many, if not most, of those who sell their risky assets at the bottom of a financial crisis do not do so because they have run out of financial liquidity. Most do not, at that single point in time, need their entire portfolios to be liquidated to fund spending. In other words, they are not insolvent; they still have risk capacity. Instead, they run out of *emotional liquidity*. They are afraid they will lose the rest of their money. Immediate behavioural risk aversion spikes, and emotional time horizons decrease to zero.

The crucial difference is that the shorter time horizon that comes with reduced risk capacity is one we *should* reflect in the optimal portfolio. Take more risk than you have capacity for and you risk financial insolvency. The shorter time horizon that stems from behavioural risk attitudes, in contrast, is one we should fight against, not embrace. Changing "optimal" portfolio risk to reflect emotional time horizons and behavioural risk attitudes takes investors away from the appropriate solution, not toward it. Of course we can't ignore the risks of emotional insolvency; when we are stressed, we crave emotional comfort at any cost and hence make costly investment decisions to acquire it. But pandering to these emotional responses is a very expensive way of sleeping better at night.

The correct solution for the *Homo economicus* version of Christy that is portrayed in Cases 1–4 is the conventional goal of finance theory: to maximise her *risk-adjusted returns*, where the adjustment for risk derives from the appropriate risk profile that results from the combination of her risk tolerance and risk capacity. The right solution for the more human Christy of Case 5 has the *same risk profile*—she has the same long-term needs and preferences—but the goal should instead be to maximise *anxiety-adjusted returns*.

The information we gather in profiling her behavioural risk attitudes is vital in understanding what makes her anxious and uncomfortable along the journey so that we may help her overcome these adverse influences on her actual risk taking. With this insight, we can help her buy the emotional comfort she requires as efficiently and cheaply as possible—that is, with as little deviation from the solution that fits her long-term risk profile as possible.

This is not to say that behavioural risk attitudes should never lead us to change the suitable risk levels, asset allocation, or individual investments in her portfolio. These may all be valid ways of reducing anxiety. For example, her ambiguity aversion might be

[22]This quote is frequently attributed to Keynes but was first recorded in the early 1990s.

assuaged by deliberately introducing some home bias, or small concentrations to familiar assets among her holdings. Doing so might be suboptimal relative to the theoretically "perfect" portfolio, but this small loss of efficiency might be well spent if it makes Christy more comfortable with investing over the long term. Similarly, dollar-cost averaging is technically inefficient and thus theoretically "wrong,"[23] but in many cases, it could be a very cheap way of giving someone the minimal emotional comfort they need to get invested at all. Maximising anxiety-adjusted returns can even be brought into a quantitative portfolio optimisation process that targets specific measures reflecting those aspects of portfolio paths that are most likely to induce anxiety.[24]

But the crucial point is that satisfying behavioural risk concerns are never the *goal* of investing and, as such, should never be used as inputs to construct the "optimal" portfolio: They are what we need to *overcome* in order to get closer to the optimal portfolio. And sometimes that means moving slightly away from the "best" solution if by doing so we purchase a big reduction in anxiety.

Do not let the best be the enemy of the good.

MAPPING THE LANDSCAPE

Bringing all the cases together, we can now discern a mapping between four reasonably distinct strands of an investor's overall situation and different aspects of his resulting profile, as shown in **Exhibit 1**. These four strands fall roughly on a continuum from purely financial to purely behavioural:

1. Financial circumstances—the investor's current balance sheet, cash flow expectations, and insurance coverage

2. Goals and aspirations—the investor's future spending goals

3. Personality traits—long-term, stable proclivities toward certain behaviours, such as risk tolerance or innate investment composure

4. Emotions and behaviour—short-term behavioural responses to context and environment

This "continuum" maps nicely to the traditional categories of *ability to take risk* (risk capacity) and *willingness to take risk*. The former largely reflects financial circumstances,

[23]On the grounds that leaving wealth uninvested when expected risk-adjusted returns are positive is suboptimal; having determined an optimal asset allocation, an alternative allocation that dilutes this with cash cannot also be optimal.
[24]See Davies and Lim (2014).

whereas the latter is more about personality. However, as discussed, future cash flows and goals can play a pivotal part in defining both ability and willingness.

We may characterise risk tolerance as the investor's long-term, stable personality preference for risk versus return. Alternatively, we can think of risk tolerance as the investor's willingness to risk attaining fewer future goals for the chance of attaining more future goals. This framing in terms of goals is helpful but not necessary: Some investors may, more simply, prefer to think of risk tolerance as the willingness to risk a certain amount of money for the possibility of earning even more money.

However, willingness to take risk also includes numerous behavioural risk attitudes: short-term behavioural responses (among others, reference dependence, framing, loss aversion, ambiguity aversion, risk perception, myopia, hyperbolic discounting, and probability distortion) that reflect both the immediate context and aspects of the investor's personality (such as her innate degree of investment *composure*).

EXHIBIT 1. INVESTMENT PLANNING USING RISK CAPACITY AND RISK TOLERANCE

<table>
<tr><th>Financial Circumstances</th><th>Goals and Aspirations</th><th>Personality Traits</th><th>Emotions and Behaviour</th></tr>
<tr><td>Ability to take risk</td><td colspan="3">Willingness to take risk</td></tr>
<tr><td>Risk capacity</td><td colspan="2">Risk tolerance</td><td>Behavioural risk attitudes</td></tr>
<tr><td colspan="3">Investor's risk profile – seek to satisfy these requirements</td><td>Seek to mitigate, not appease</td></tr>
</table>

Exhibit 1 sums up these ideas. The final row shows that risk capacity and risk tolerance together form essential components of the appropriate (or suitable) risk level for an investor's overall investable assets. Behavioural risk attitudes, however, while also essential to understand, reflect not the risk an investor *should* take but, rather, the emotional currents that constantly pull investors off the appropriate path along the investment journey. They need to be mitigated, neutralised, or overcome—and sometimes, to as small a degree as possible, appeased. But they should never be mistaken for the right answer.

Much of the confusion surrounding current risk-profiling practices stems from a lack of clarity about the boundaries between these concepts—in particular, the following:

1. Undue focus on risk tolerance at the expense of understanding risk capacity (measuring what can be measured most easily), making risk tolerance do more of the work than it should in determining suitability

2. Confusion between risk tolerance and behavioural risk attitudes, with a tendency to want to treat observations of the latter as a proxy for the former

3. A lack of any clear model of risk capacity that truly accounts for the full range of influencing factors—specifically, a failure to understand the crucial role that investor goals play in an adequate description of risk capacity or the fundamental importance of imprecision, fuzziness, and adaptability of these goals

4. Failing to realise that the true suitability of an investment solution can be demonstrated only in the context of the investor's overall situation—neither risk tolerance nor risk capacity can be intelligibly measured for isolated components of an investor's wealth

NEW VISTAS

So given this landscape, how can we better set about the practical process of effective risk profiling?

Comprehensive descriptions of risk capacity models and goal-based investing would each require an article of their own (at least). However, it is fair to say that each of these requires vastly greater attention than they currently receive. Here I shall focus on the narrower question of measuring attitudes.

MEASURING RISK TOLERANCE

A corollary to the lack of focus on risk capacity is that little would be lost by sticking to simple psychometric approaches to measuring risk tolerance. There is an unnecessary tendency to want to overcomplicate this easiest-to-measure aspect of an investor's risk profile. Efforts to pour more resources into ever more sophisticated ways of eliciting risk tolerance are to a large degree unnecessary and in many cases misguided. There is a danger of spurious precision in risk tolerance measurement, and in striving for greater precision, there is a concern that we measure revealed preferences and observed behaviours that are more properly reflective of behavioural risk attitudes than of true risk tolerance.[25]

Measured correctly, decent psychometric measures of risk tolerance are stable and differentiate effectively and reliably between individual investors. The gap lies not in how risk tolerance is measured but in how it is used. A simple, well-designed measure, used well, is hard to beat.

[25]A discussion of existing methodologies for eliciting risk attitudes may be found in Egan, Davies, and Brooks (2011).

That said, there are enticing opportunities for measuring risk tolerance in ways that offer a better client experience and greater accuracy. One is making existing psychometric questionnaires more dynamic, making the questioning process more responsive to existing client knowledge and initial responses, and gleaning more information out of fewer questions.

This *might* be supplemented with asking clients to respond to explicit hypothetical choices (for example, presenting them with choices between investment options or combinations of risk and return) and visual stimuli, using pictures rather than questions. However, such approaches often give very momentary readings of how an investor responds to specific questions and may not offer generalizable insights, instead providing only overly precise estimates that hold true only in these hypothetical, and often highly artificial, situations. It will be crucial to validate the idea that such tools correlate strongly to existing psychometric risk tolerance measures.

A further area of promise is to use big data, observed behavioural patterns, and machine learning to home in on an investor's risk tolerance. Such data have been very effective in assessing numerous personality traits,[26] and since risk tolerance is best understood as a personality trait, it could well lend itself to these techniques. However, there are valid concerns about data protection with many of these applications, and in deploying such techniques, it is crucial that we are able to clearly discern between risk tolerance and behavioural risk attitudes.

On balance, anything more complicated than a simple well-designed and validated psychometric questionnaire is likely to be both unnecessary and less robust.

MEASURING BEHAVIOURAL RISK ATTITUDES

Unearthing unstable behavioural risk attitudes is where observing real behaviour has the greatest potential. Behavioural responses are complex, individual, and unpredictable. As long as methods to measure them are used thoughtfully and intelligently, observing patterns of changing attitudes to risk may well help in guiding investors to better behaviour along the journey. These profiling techniques may include both psychometric instruments and observing historical behaviour. Each provides valuable insight on what makes investors anxious and uncomfortable. By examining how investors really respond to a wide range of actual situations, we can start to build a rich profile of their behavioural tendencies and identify spots where these are likely to be costly.

[26]For example, the myPersonality project of the Cambridge University Psychometrics Centre, in which correlations between individuals' online Facebook profiles and their personality traits are studied.

With knowledge of the investor's full balance sheet and armed with systems describing the cash flows and (imprecise) goals required for risk capacity, another option becomes possible. Rather than just looking at history, which exposes investors to only a limited range of all the possible events they might have to bear, we could instead expose investors to simulated versions of their future financial lives and use responses to these as profiling inputs. Even more valuably, such risk simulations have been shown to improve long-term investment decisions[27] and thus can be used to educate and prepare investors for the future.

This points to where profiling is potentially most valuable with regard to behavioural risk attitudes: Profiling should provide an opportunity for investors to learn about their attitudes, emotions, and biases, and in doing so, it should help them prepare for the anxiety of the journey.[28] The more this can be done using investors' own past behaviour and their specific financial situation and goals, the more effectively it will help them to take and stick with the right amount of risk.

DYNAMIC PROFILING

Possibly the most exciting new vista in risk profiling is not about the specifics of what is being measured; rather, it is in when and how the data are collected and used. At present, suitability, client fact-finding, and profiling approaches can be off-putting. The conventional presumption is that a comprehensive profile is needed from the outset, so clients are often exposed to a great deal of questioning up front. This situation results in a poor client experience and poor subsequent commitment, as well as in advisers cutting corners and "box-ticking" in order to hasten the process. Little is gained in terms of client education or emotional preparation for investing. And the solution arrived at is then often over-fitted to the client's circumstances, opinions, and emotional state at that one specific point in time. This solution is then regarded as the right ongoing solution, sometimes for many years, despite constant shifts in the investor's portfolio, circumstances, preferences, and goals.

Instead, we need to use advances in technology, data analytics, and behavioural design (in particular, techniques from *gamification* to help investors engage comfortably with complex systems[29]) to blur the current distinctions between *profiling*, *suitability*, and *client engagement*. The initial process should be as minimal, simple, and easy for the investor as possible. The more effort it takes to start investing, the more investors

---

[27]Bradbury, Hens, and Zeisberger (2016).

[28]"Beyond Risk Profiling" (2015).

[29]Note that by "gamification," I do *not* mean turning the process into a game or trivializing it. Instead, gamification is, or should be, the use of tools and techniques (often borrowed from, or used in, the gaming industry) to lead people rapidly and comfortably to sophisticated patterns of behaviour that enable them to engage effectively with complex environments or problems.

(particularly first time investors) are put off. However, after starting, advisers should be constantly profiling.

Every engagement point is an opportunity to enrich the profile—to ask the few next questions that offer the most value in deepening customer understanding. Every change in the profile offers an opportunity to sharpen the overall advisory solution: either directly through changing the portfolio (although here the range of options to respond to small changes in the profile is relatively constrained) or indirectly by changing how we engage and communicate with the client, how we manage clients' emotional states over the journey, how we plan and program future actions and responses, how we report performance, and how we involve the client in ongoing decisions. And every change to the overall solution is an opportunity to identify new valuable engagement opportunities. This approach conceives of risk profiling as part of a never-ending dialogue between investor and adviser, constantly updating the profile to gather more information and adapt to changes in circumstances and preferences.

The risk tolerance measure at the heart of the profile remains the steady core around which the profile is built and will in all likelihood still be most effectively arrived at through a simple psychometric questionnaire at the start of the investment relationship (and which is refreshed occasionally). But once the basics are in place and clients have invested, their risk capacity, goals, and behavioural risk attitudes can become an entirely dynamic process, both adapting and deepening through the client relationship. Of course this is much how human advisers' subjective understanding of their clients' needs deepens over time. But with advanced data analytics, gamification, and machine learning, we are coming to the point where we can blur the distinction between formal profiling and an adviser's client understanding, ultimately creating a profiling process as a digital *decision prosthetic* to supplement and enhance the essential human side of investing.

In conclusion, if we want to move forward in risk profiling as an industry, we should resist the temptation to focus on ever more complex batteries of questions to elicit and parameterise complex approaches to risk tolerance. Simple is best. We should instead focus on building and improving dynamic models of risk capacity and tools to truly help investors understand and articulate their own goals without requiring that they express these goals with any greater precision than that with which they are truly held. We should concentrate much more on how we *use* this knowledge and include simple risk tolerance measures in coherent suitability frameworks that reflect an understanding of what truly matters to clients. And, finally, we should stop treating profiling as a single point-in-time activity, divorced from the ongoing client relationship, but instead ensure that suitability adjusts dynamically to meet constantly changing needs.

The ultimate new vista in risk profiling is that it becomes impossible to separate from goal-based suitability and effective client engagement.

REFERENCES

Benartzi, S., and R. Thaler. 1995. "Myopic Loss Aversion and the Equity Premium Puzzle." *Quarterly Journal of Economics*, vol. 110, no. 1: 73–92.

"Beyond Risk Profiling: Achieving Better Investment Outcomes for Consumers and Industry." 2015. White paper, True Potential Centre for the Public Understanding of Finance (October).

Bradbury, M., T. Hens, and S. Zeisberger. 2016. "Do Risk Simulations Lead to Persistently Better Investment Decisions?" Working paper (12 July).

Brooks, P., G.B. Davies, and R.E.D. Smith. 2015. "A Behavioral Perspective on Goal-Based Investing." *Investments & Wealth Monitor* (November/December).

Davies, G.B. 2014. "Overcoming the Cost of Being Human." White paper, Barclays.

Davies, G.B., and P. Brooks. 2014. "Risk Tolerance: Essential, Behavioural, and Misunderstood." *Journal of Risk Management in Financial Institutions*, vol. 7, no. 2 (Spring): 110–113.

Davies, G.B., and A. de Servigny. 2012. *Behavioral Investment Management: An Efficient Alternative to Modern Portfolio Theory*. McGraw-Hill Professional.

Davies, G.B., and A. Lim. 2014. "Managing Anxiety to Improve Financial Performance: Don't Let the Best Be the Enemy of the Achievable." In *Quantitative Approaches to High Net Worth Investment*. Edited by A. Rudd and S. Satchell. London: Risk Books.

Egan, D., G.B. Davies, and P. Brooks. 2011. "Comparisons of Risk Attitudes across Individuals." In *Wiley Encyclopedia of Operations Research and Management Science*. Wiley.

Odean, T. 1999. "Do Investors Trade Too Much?" *American Economic Review*, vol. 89, no. 5 (December): 1279–1298. doi:10.1257/aer.89.5.1279

Payne, J.W., J.R. Bettman, and D.A. Schkade. 1999. "Measuring Constructed Preferences: Towards a Building Code." *Journal of Risk and Uncertainty*, vol. 19, no. 1–3: 243–270. doi:10.1023/A:1007843931054

Rabin, M. 2000. "Risk Aversion and Expected-Utility Theory: A Calibration Theorem." *Econometrica*, vol. 68, no. 5: 1281–1292.

Sahm, C.R. 2012. "How Much Does Risk Tolerance Change?" *Quarterly Journal of Finance*, vol. 2, no. 4 (December).

Samuelson, P.A. 1963. "Risk and Uncertainty: A Fallacy of Large Numbers." *Scientia*, vol. 98 (April/May): 108–113.

Slovic, P. 1995. "The Construction of Preference." *American Psychologist*, vol. 50, no. 5 (May): 364–371.

Thaler, R.H. 1999. "Mental Accounting Matters." *Journal of Behavioral Decision Making*, vol. 12: 183–206.

Weber, M., E.U. Weber, and A. Nosić. 2013. "Who Takes Risks When and Why: Determinants of Changes in Investor Risk Taking." *Review of Finance*, vol. 17 (July): 847–883.

Named Endowments

CFA Institute Research Foundation acknowledges with sincere gratitude the generous contributions of the Named Endowment participants listed below.

Gifts of at least US$100,000 qualify donors for membership in the Named Endowment category, which recognizes in perpetuity the commitment toward unbiased, practitioner-oriented, relevant research that these firms and individuals have expressed through their generous support of the CFA Institute Research Foundation.

Ameritech
Anonymous
Robert D. Arnott
Theodore R. Aronson, CFA
Asahi Mutual Life Insurance Company
Batterymarch Financial Management
Boston Company
Boston Partners Asset Management, L.P.
Gary P. Brinson, CFA
Brinson Partners, Inc.
Capital Group International, Inc.
Concord Capital Management
Dai-Ichi Life Insurance Company
Daiwa Securities
Mr. and Mrs. Jeffrey Diermeier
Gifford Fong Associates
John A. Gunn, CFA
Investment Counsel Association of America, Inc.
Jacobs Levy Equity Management
Jon L. Hagler Foundation
Long-Term Credit Bank of Japan, Ltd.
Lynch, Jones & Ryan, LLC
Meiji Mutual Life Insurance Company
Miller Anderson & Sherrerd, LLP
John B. Neff, CFA
Nikko Securities Co., Ltd.
Nippon Life Insurance Company of Japan
Nomura Securities Co., Ltd.
Payden & Rygel
Provident National Bank
Frank K. Reilly, CFA
Salomon Brothers
Sassoon Holdings Pte. Ltd.
Scudder Stevens & Clark
Security Analysts Association of Japan
Shaw Data Securities, Inc.
Sit Investment Associates, Inc.
Standish, Ayer & Wood, Inc.
State Farm Insurance Company
Sumitomo Life America, Inc.
T. Rowe Price Associates, Inc.
Templeton Investment Counsel Inc.
Frank Trainer, CFA
Travelers Insurance Co.
USF&G Companies
Yamaichi Securities Co., Ltd.

Senior Research Fellows

Financial Services Analyst Association

For more on upcoming Research Foundation publications and webcasts, please visit www.cfainstitute.org/learning/foundation.

Research Foundation monographs are online at www.cfapubs.org.

Made in the USA
Monee, IL
05 November 2026

67378078R00067